REUNITING FAMILIES THROUGH RESTORATIVE JUSTICE

Dr. Maxwell Shimba

Shimba Publishing, LLC.

Printed in the United States of America

TABLE OF CONTENTS

INTRODUCTION

What is Restorative Justice?

Restorative justice is a philosophy and an approach to justice that emphasizes healing the harm caused by criminal behavior. It involves all stakeholders, including victims, offenders, and the community, in a process that promotes repair, reconciliation, and the rebuilding of relationships. This chapter will explore the concept of restorative justice from three distinct perspectives: theological, psychological, and philosophical.

1. Theologically

Biblical Foundations

Restorative justice finds strong support in various religious traditions, particularly within Christianity. The Bible presents numerous examples of restorative practices, emphasizing reconciliation, forgiveness, and the restoration of relationships. For instance, the story of Zacchaeus in the New Testament illustrates restorative justice principles. When Zacchaeus, a tax collector, repents and offers restitution to those he has wronged, Jesus proclaims that salvation has come to his house (Luke 19:1-10).

Theological Principles

1. Reconciliation: Central to Christian theology is the concept of reconciliation. The Apostle Paul speaks of the ministry of reconciliation, urging believers to be reconciled to God and to each other (2 Corinthians 5:18-20). Restorative justice mirrors this divine call by seeking to reconcile victims and offenders.

2. Forgiveness: Forgiveness is a cornerstone of Christian teaching. Jesus' teachings, particularly the Lord's Prayer, emphasize the importance of forgiving others as we have been forgiven (Matthew 6:12-15). Restorative justice encourages offenders to seek forgiveness and victims to offer it, fostering a spirit of healing and renewal.

3. Restoration: The concept of shalom, or peace, in the Hebrew Bible encompasses wholeness, completeness, and restoration. Restorative justice aims to restore relationships and communities to a state of wholeness, reflecting the biblical vision of peace.

Practical Applications

In practice, restorative justice in a theological context may involve church-led mediation sessions, community reconciliation programs, and spiritual counseling. These initiatives focus on healing relationships and addressing the spiritual needs of those involved in the justice process.

2. Psychologically

Impact on Victims

From a psychological perspective, restorative justice offers significant benefits to victims of crime. Traditional justice systems often leave victims feeling marginalized and unheard. In contrast, restorative justice provides a platform for victims to express their emotions, share their experiences, and participate actively in the justice process.

1. Empowerment: Restorative justice empowers victims by giving them a voice. This empowerment can lead to a sense of closure and a reduction in feelings of helplessness and anxiety.

2. Emotional Healing: The process of sharing one's story and receiving acknowledgment from the offender can be therapeutic. It allows victims to process their trauma and begin the healing journey.

3. Validation: Victims often seek validation of their suffering. Restorative justice acknowledges their pain and validates their experiences, fostering a sense of justice and fairness.

Impact on Offenders

Restorative justice also has profound psychological effects on offenders. Traditional punitive measures may lead to feelings of resentment and recidivism. In contrast, restorative justice encourages personal growth and transformation.

1. Accountability: By facing their victims and understanding the impact of their actions, offenders are held accountable in a meaningful way. This accountability can lead to genuine remorse and a desire to make amends.

2. Personal Growth: The process encourages offenders to reflect on their behavior, understand the root causes of their actions, and commit to positive change. This can lead to reduced recidivism and better integration into society.

3. Restoration of Self-Worth: Restorative justice promotes the idea that offenders are more than their crimes. It focuses on their potential for rehabilitation and reintegration, restoring their sense of self-worth.

Impact on Communities

Psychologically, restorative justice also benefits communities by promoting social cohesion and collective healing. It addresses the broader impact of crime on the community and fosters a supportive environment for both victims and offenders.

3. Philosophically

Philosophical Foundations

Restorative justice is grounded in several key philosophical principles that distinguish it from retributive justice systems.

1. Relational Justice: At its core, restorative justice views crime as a violation of relationships rather than merely a breach of law. This relational perspective emphasizes the interconnectedness of individuals within a community.

2. Holistic Approach: Restorative justice takes a holistic approach to justice, considering the needs of victims, offenders, and the community. It seeks to address the root causes of criminal behavior and promote overall well-being.

3. Focus on Harm: Unlike retributive justice, which focuses on punishing the offender, restorative justice focuses on the harm caused by the crime and the steps needed to repair it. This harm-centric approach aims to restore balance and harmony.

Ethical Considerations

1. Restorative Ethics: The ethical foundation of restorative justice is built on principles of respect, empathy, and compassion. It seeks to treat all parties with dignity and fairness, fostering a culture of mutual respect.

2. Justice as Healing: Restorative justice redefines justice as a process of healing rather than punishment. This philosophical shift challenges conventional notions of justice and promotes a more humane and compassionate approach.

3. Community Responsibility: Philosophically, restorative justice emphasizes the role of the community in the justice process. It advocates for collective responsibility in addressing crime and supporting both victims and offenders.

Practical Applications

Philosophical principles of restorative justice can be applied in various settings, including schools, workplaces, and the criminal justice system. Restorative practices such as mediation, circle processes, and community conferencing are practical applications that embody these philosophical ideals.

Conclusion

Restorative justice is a multifaceted approach that integrates theological, psychological, and philosophical perspectives to create a more holistic and humane justice system. By focusing on healing, accountability, and community involvement, restorative justice offers a transformative alternative to traditional punitive measures. This chapter has explored the foundational principles and benefits of restorative justice, setting the stage for a deeper understanding of its application in reuniting families and fostering peace.

DR. MAXWELL SHIMBA

CHAPTER 01

THE IMPORTANCE OF FAMILY REUNIFICATION

Families are the fundamental units of society, providing support, love, and stability to their members. When a crime occurs, it can have a devastating impact on the family structure, leading to broken relationships, mistrust, and emotional trauma. Restorative justice seeks to address these impacts by facilitating dialogue, understanding, and ultimately, healing. This chapter will explore the importance of family reunification in the context of restorative justice and how it can help mend broken relationships, provide emotional support, and foster a supportive environment for all involved.

Emotional and Psychological Impacts of Crime on Families

Emotional Trauma

Crime can cause significant emotional trauma for families. Victims often experience feelings of fear, anger, and betrayal, while offenders may feel guilt, shame, and isolation. Family members who are neither victims nor offenders can also suffer, as they navigate the fallout and attempt to support their loved ones.

1. Fear and Anxiety: Families may live in constant fear of further harm or retribution. This anxiety can affect their daily lives and mental health.

2. Anger and Resentment: Victims and their families may harbor deep resentment towards the offender, which can create lasting divisions within the family unit.

3. Shame and Isolation: Offenders and their families often face social stigma, leading to feelings of shame and isolation from their community.

Psychological Healing through Restorative Justice

Restorative justice offers a pathway to psychological healing by providing a safe space for all parties to express their emotions and seek closure.

1. Acknowledgment of Harm: Victims have the opportunity to convey the impact of the crime on their lives, which can be validating and cathartic.

2. Empathy and Understanding: Offenders can gain a deeper understanding of the consequences of their actions, fostering empathy and remorse.

3. Mutual Support: Families can come together to support one another through the healing process, strengthening their bonds.

Rebuilding Trust and Relationships

The Role of Dialogue

Open and honest dialogue is crucial for rebuilding trust and relationships within families affected by crime. Restorative justice provides a structured environment for such dialogue to take place.

1. Safe Space for Communication: Facilitated meetings ensure that all parties can speak freely without fear of judgment or retaliation.

2. Active Listening: Participants are encouraged to listen actively and empathetically, fostering mutual understanding and respect.

3. Constructive Feedback: Offenders can receive constructive feedback on how their actions have affected their loved ones, helping them to take responsibility and make amends.

Steps to Mend Broken Relationships

1. Acknowledgment of Wrongdoing: Offenders must acknowledge their wrongdoing and understand its impact on the family.

2. Apology and Forgiveness: A sincere apology from the offender can pave the way for forgiveness from the victim and other family members.

3. Commitment to Change: Offenders must demonstrate a commitment to change their behavior and rebuild trust through consistent, positive actions.

The Role of Restorative Justice Conferencing

What is Restorative Justice Conferencing?

Restorative justice conferencing is a key practice in facilitating family reunification. It involves structured meetings between victims, offenders, and their families to discuss the crime's impact and agree on steps to repair the harm.

1. Facilitated Dialogue: A trained facilitator guides the conversation, ensuring that it remains respectful and productive.

2. Inclusive Participation: All affected family members are encouraged to participate, share their perspectives, and contribute to the resolution process.

3. Collaborative Decision-Making: The group works together to develop a plan for repairing the harm and moving forward.

Benefits of Restorative Justice Conferencing

1. Empowerment of Victims: Victims have a platform to voice their experiences and needs, which can be empowering and healing.

2. Responsibility and Accountability: Offenders are held accountable in a meaningful way, encouraging them to take responsibility and make amends.

3. Strengthened Family Bonds: The process can strengthen family bonds by fostering understanding, empathy, and mutual support.

Case Studies of Family Reunification through Restorative Justice

Case Study 1: Healing after Theft

In a case where a family member committed theft against another family member, restorative justice conferencing provided a platform for the offender to apologize and make restitution. The victim expressed their pain and the impact of the theft, while the offender acknowledged their wrongdoing and committed to making amends. This process led to a renewed sense of trust and a strengthened family bond.

Case Study 2: Reconciliation after Domestic Violence

A case involving domestic violence demonstrated the potential of restorative justice to facilitate healing and reconciliation. Through facilitated dialogue, the victim expressed their trauma, and the offender took responsibility for their actions. With ongoing support and counseling, the family began to rebuild their relationship on a foundation of trust and mutual respect.

Case Study 3: Restoring Community Trust

In a community-wide incident affecting multiple families, restorative justice conferencing helped to restore trust and relationships. Community members came together to share their experiences, understand the broader impact of the crime, and develop collective solutions to prevent future incidents.

Practical Steps to Implement Family Reunification

Preparation and Assessment

1. Screening for Suitability: Assessing whether restorative justice conferencing is appropriate for the family and the specific crime.

2. Preparation of Participants: Ensuring that all participants are prepared for the process, understand its goals, and are willing to engage constructively.

Conducting the Conference

1. Facilitator's Role: The facilitator guides the process, ensuring that it remains respectful and focused on healing.

2. Structure of the Conference: The conference typically follows a structured format, including introductions, sharing of experiences, discussion of the impact, and development of a resolution plan.

Follow-Up and Support

1. Ongoing Support: Providing continued support for families after the conference to ensure that the agreements are implemented and that relationships continue to heal.

2. Monitoring Progress: Regular check-ins to monitor progress and address any emerging issues or challenges.

Conclusion

Family reunification is a crucial aspect of restorative justice, offering a pathway to healing and rebuilding relationships affected by crime. By facilitating dialogue, understanding, and mutual support, restorative justice helps to mend broken relationships, provide emotional healing, and foster a supportive environment for all involved. This chapter has highlighted the importance of family reunification, the role of restorative justice conferencing, and practical steps to implement these practices, setting the stage for a deeper exploration of restorative justice in subsequent chapters.

Objectives of the Book

This book aims to explore the concept of restorative justice, with a particular focus on family reunification through conferencing. It will provide a comprehensive overview of the philosophy, principles, and practical applications of restorative justice. Additionally, it will offer insights into the challenges and successes of restorative justice conferencing and its potential to bring peace and healing to families affected by crime.

Comprehensive Overview of Restorative Justice

One of the primary objectives of this book is to provide readers with a thorough understanding of restorative justice. This includes its origins, key principles, and how it differs from traditional punitive approaches to justice. By delving into the philosophical, psychological, and theological underpinnings of restorative justice, readers will gain a holistic view of this transformative approach.

Focus on Family Reunification

Family reunification is a central theme of this book. Crime can fracture family relationships, leading to long-term emotional and psychological damage. This book will explore how restorative justice, particularly through conferencing, can help mend these broken relationships. By facilitating dialogue, understanding, and healing, restorative justice aims to bring families back together and foster a supportive environment for all involved.

Practical Applications of Restorative Justice

Beyond theory, this book will provide practical insights into the implementation of restorative justice practices. It will explore various models of restorative justice conferencing, such as victim-offender mediation, family group conferencing, and community conferencing. Through real-life case studies and examples, readers will see how these practices can be applied in different contexts to achieve positive outcomes.

Insights into Challenges and Successes

Implementing restorative justice is not without its challenges. This book will address common obstacles, such as resistance from participants, power imbalances, and safety concerns. It will also offer strategies and best practices for overcoming these challenges to ensure successful outcomes. Furthermore, the book will highlight the successes of restorative justice conferencing, showcasing how it has brought peace and healing to families affected by crime.

Potential for Peace and Healing

Ultimately, this book aims to demonstrate the profound potential of restorative justice to bring peace and healing to families and communities. By focusing on repairing harm, fostering empathy, and promoting accountability, restorative justice offers a pathway to reconciliation and transformation. This book will inspire readers to consider restorative justice as a viable and effective alternative to traditional punitive approaches, particularly in the context of family reunification.

Conclusion

The objectives of this book are to provide a comprehensive understanding of restorative justice, with a special focus on family reunification through conferencing. By exploring the philosophy, principles, and practical applications of restorative justice, and addressing the challenges and successes of its implementation, this book aims to inspire and inform readers about the transformative potential of restorative justice. Through the stories and insights shared, readers will gain a deeper appreciation for how restorative justice can bring peace and healing to families affected by crime.

CHAPTER 02

THE PHILOSOPHY OF RESTORATIVE JUSTICE

Understanding Justice

Traditional justice systems often focus on punishment and retribution. In contrast, restorative justice emphasizes repairing harm, restoring relationships, and reintegrating offenders into society. This chapter explores the foundational principles that distinguish restorative justice from conventional justice systems.

Traditional Justice Systems

Punishment and Retribution

Traditional justice systems are primarily retributive in nature. They operate on the principle that crime is a violation of the law, and the primary response should be punishment. This approach seeks to deter crime through the fear of punishment and to incapacitate offenders to prevent further harm.

1. Focus on the Offender: Traditional systems focus on the offender's guilt and the appropriate punishment. The needs of victims and the community are often secondary considerations.

2. Adversarial Process: The justice process is adversarial, pitting the prosecution against the defense in a contest to establish guilt or innocence. This can lead to further animosity and conflict.

3. Punitive Measures: Sentences often involve incarceration, fines, or other punitive measures designed to punish the offender rather than address the underlying causes of the behavior or repair the harm done.

The Principles of Restorative Justice

Repairing Harm

At the core of restorative justice is the principle of repairing harm. Crime is seen as a violation of people and relationships, not just a breach of law. The primary goal is to repair the harm caused by the offense.

1. Victim-Centered Approach: Restorative justice prioritizes the needs and experiences of the victim. Victims are given a voice in the process and their needs are addressed directly.

2. Accountability and Responsibility: Offenders are encouraged to take responsibility for their actions and to understand the impact of their behavior on the victim and the community.

3. Reparation and Restoration: Efforts are made to repair the harm through restitution, apologies, community service, or other means agreed upon by the parties involved.

Restoring Relationships

Restorative justice emphasizes the importance of restoring relationships damaged by crime. This involves not only the relationship between the victim and the offender but also the broader social relationships within the community.

1. Inclusive Dialogue: Restorative justice practices, such as conferencing and circles, involve open dialogue among all affected parties. This inclusive process fosters understanding and empathy.

2. Community Involvement: The community plays a central role in supporting the victim, holding the offender accountable, and facilitating the restoration of relationships.

3. Healing and Reconciliation: The ultimate goal is to achieve healing and reconciliation, allowing all parties to move forward in a positive and constructive manner.

Reintegration of Offenders

Restorative justice seeks to reintegrate offenders into society rather than isolate them. This approach recognizes the potential for personal growth and transformation.

1. Supportive Environment: Offenders are supported in their efforts to make amends and reintegrate into the community. This support can include counseling, education, and vocational training.

2. Transformative Justice: The process aims to transform offenders by addressing the underlying causes of their behavior, such as social, economic, or psychological factors.

3. Reduction of Recidivism: By focusing on rehabilitation and reintegration, restorative justice aims to reduce recidivism and promote long-term public safety.

Key Practices in Restorative Justice

Victim-Offender Mediation

Victim-offender mediation is a facilitated process that allows victims and offenders to communicate directly. This practice provides a safe space for victims to express their feelings and for offenders to take responsibility for their actions.

1. Preparation: Both parties are prepared for the mediation process, ensuring they understand the goals and are willing to participate constructively.

2. Facilitated Dialogue: A trained mediator facilitates the dialogue, helping to navigate difficult emotions and ensure that the conversation remains productive.

3. Agreement: The parties work together to reach an agreement on how to repair the harm. This agreement may include restitution, community service, or other forms of reparation.

Family Group Conferencing

Family group conferencing involves the extended family and support networks of both the victim and the offender. This practice recognizes the role of family and community in the healing process.

1. Family Involvement: Family members and supporters are actively involved in the process, providing emotional support and contributing to the resolution.

2. Collective Decision-Making: The group works together to develop a plan for repairing the harm and supporting the offender's reintegration.

3. Strengthening Bonds: The process helps to strengthen family and community bonds, promoting a sense of collective responsibility and support.

Community Conferencing

Community conferencing involves a broader group of community members who are affected by the crime. This practice aims to address the wider impact of crime on the community and to involve the community in the justice process.

1. Community Participation: Community members participate in the process, sharing their perspectives and contributing to the resolution.

2. Collective Healing: The process promotes collective healing by addressing the harm caused to the community and fostering a sense of solidarity.

3. Building Community Resilience: By involving the community in the justice process, restorative justice helps to build community resilience and cohesion.

Ethical Considerations in Restorative Justice

Respect and Dignity

Restorative justice operates on principles of respect and dignity for all participants. This ethical foundation ensures that everyone is treated with fairness and compassion.

1. Respect for Victims: Victims are respected and their experiences and needs are prioritized.

2. Respect for Offenders: Offenders are treated with dignity and given the opportunity to take responsibility and make amends.

3. Inclusive Process: The process is inclusive, ensuring that all voices are heard and respected.

Fairness and Equity

Restorative justice seeks to achieve fairness and equity in the justice process. This involves addressing power imbalances and ensuring that all parties have an equal opportunity to participate.

1. Addressing Power Imbalances: Facilitators work to address power imbalances and ensure that all participants can engage meaningfully.

2. Equitable Outcomes: The process aims to achieve outcomes that are fair and equitable for all parties involved.

3. Transparency and Accountability: The process is transparent, with clear communication and accountability at every stage.

Conclusion

Restorative justice represents a transformative approach to justice that focuses on repairing harm, restoring relationships, and reintegrating offenders into society. By prioritizing the needs and experiences of victims, promoting accountability and responsibility among offenders, and involving the community in the justice process, restorative justice offers a holistic and humane alternative to traditional punitive systems. This chapter has explored the foundational principles of restorative justice, highlighting its potential to create a more just and compassionate society. Subsequent chapters will delve deeper into the practical applications and case studies of restorative justice, providing further insights into its impact and effectiveness.

Healing over Punishment

Restorative justice is centered on the core value of healing over punishment. This approach emphasizes the well-being of victims and communities rather than merely punishing offenders. By prioritizing healing, restorative justice seeks to address the harm caused by crime and foster reconciliation and transformation for all involved. This chapter delves into the philosophy, benefits, and practical applications of prioritizing healing over punishment in the justice process.

The Philosophy of Healing over Punishment

Understanding Healing

Healing in the context of restorative justice refers to the process of addressing the emotional, psychological, and relational harm caused by crime. It involves restoring a sense of safety, trust, and well-being for victims, offenders, and the community.

1. Emotional Restoration: Healing involves helping victims process their emotions, such as fear, anger, and betrayal, and supporting them in finding closure.

2. Psychological Support: Providing psychological support to both victims and offenders helps them cope with trauma and fosters mental well-being.

3. Relational Repair: Healing focuses on repairing broken relationships, fostering empathy, and rebuilding trust among affected parties.

The Limitations of Punishment

Traditional punitive justice systems focus on retribution, aiming to deter crime through fear of punishment and incapacitate offenders. However, this approach has several limitations.

1. Lack of Closure for Victims: Punitive measures often do not address the emotional and psychological needs of victims, leaving them without a sense of closure or healing.

2. Increased Recidivism: Punishment alone does not address the root causes of criminal behavior, leading to high rates of recidivism as offenders are not given the tools to change.

3. Community Alienation: Punitive justice can alienate offenders from their communities, hindering their reintegration and perpetuating cycles of crime.

Benefits of Prioritizing Healing

For Victims

1. Empowerment: Restorative justice empowers victims by giving them a voice in the justice process and addressing their needs and concerns directly.

2. Emotional Healing: By participating in restorative practices, victims can express their emotions, receive validation, and find closure, aiding in their emotional healing.

3. Restored Sense of Safety: Addressing the harm and working towards repair helps victims feel safer and more supported by their community.

For Offenders

1. Accountability and Growth: Restorative justice encourages offenders to take responsibility for their actions, fostering personal growth and transformation.

2. Reduced Recidivism: By addressing the underlying causes of criminal behavior and promoting rehabilitation, restorative justice helps reduce the likelihood of reoffending.

3. Reintegration: Focusing on healing facilitates the reintegration of offenders into their communities, allowing them to rebuild their lives and contribute positively.

For Communities

1. Strengthened Social Bonds: Restorative justice fosters community involvement and support, strengthening social bonds and promoting collective healing.

2. Increased Trust: By prioritizing healing and fairness, restorative justice builds trust in the justice system and among community members.

3. Enhanced Public Safety: A focus on rehabilitation and reintegration contributes to long-term public safety by addressing the root causes of crime and reducing recidivism.

Practical Applications of Healing over Punishment

Victim-Offender Mediation

Victim-offender mediation is a key restorative practice that emphasizes healing over punishment. It involves facilitated dialogue between victims and offenders, allowing them to discuss the impact of the crime and agree on steps to repair the harm.

1. Preparation: Both parties are prepared for the mediation process, ensuring they understand its goals and are willing to engage constructively.

2. Facilitated Dialogue: A trained mediator guides the conversation, helping to navigate difficult emotions and ensure that the dialogue remains productive.

3. Agreement on Reparation: The parties work together to reach an agreement on how to repair the harm,

which may include restitution, community service, or other forms of reparation.

Family Group Conferencing

Family group conferencing involves the extended family and support networks of both the victim and the offender. This practice recognizes the role of family and community in the healing process.

1. Inclusion of Support Networks: Family members and supporters are actively involved in the process, providing emotional support and contributing to the resolution.

2. Collaborative Decision-Making: The group works together to develop a plan for repairing the harm and supporting the offender's reintegration.

3. Strengthening Family Bonds: The process helps to strengthen family and community bonds, promoting a sense of collective responsibility and support.

Community Conferencing

Community conferencing involves a broader group of community members who are affected by the crime. This practice aims to address the wider impact of crime on the community and to involve the community in the justice process.

1. Community Participation: Community members participate in the process, sharing their perspectives and contributing to the resolution.

2. Collective Healing: The process promotes collective healing by addressing the harm caused to the community and fostering a sense of solidarity.

3. Building Resilience: By involving the community in the justice process, restorative justice helps to build community resilience and cohesion.

Case Studies Illustrating Healing over Punishment

Case Study 1: Reconciliation after Burglary

In a case involving a burglary, the victim and offender participated in a restorative justice conference. The victim was able to express the fear and violation they felt, while the offender took responsibility for their actions and apologized. The process led to an agreement on restitution and community service, fostering healing and reconciliation.

Case Study 2: Healing after Domestic Violence

A family affected by domestic violence engaged in restorative justice practices. Through facilitated dialogue, the victim shared their trauma, and the offender acknowledged their wrongdoing and committed to change. Ongoing support and counseling were provided, helping the family to heal and rebuild their relationships.

Case Study 3: Community Healing After Vandalism

In a community affected by vandalism, restorative justice conferencing brings together the offenders, victims, and community members. The dialogue helped to repair the relationships within the community, with the offenders agreeing to repair the damage and participate in community service. This process strengthened community bonds and promoted a sense of collective responsibility.

Challenges and Solutions

Resistance to Restorative Practices

1. Overcoming Skepticism: Educating stakeholders about the benefits of restorative justice can help overcome skepticism and resistance.

2. Building Trust: Establishing trust among participants is crucial. Facilitators play a key role in creating a safe and respectful environment for dialogue.

3. Providing Support: Ongoing support for victims, offenders, and community members is essential to ensure the success of restorative practices.

Ensuring Fairness and Equity

1. Addressing Power Imbalances: Facilitators must be trained to recognize and address power imbalances to ensure that all voices are heard and respected.

2. Maintaining Neutrality: Facilitators must remain neutral and impartial, focusing on the needs and well-being of all participants.

3. Inclusive Practices: Restorative justice practices should be inclusive, ensuring that all affected parties have an opportunity to participate meaningfully.

Conclusion

Healing over punishment is a foundational value of restorative justice that prioritizes the well-being of victims, offenders, and communities. By focusing on healing, restorative justice addresses the harm caused by crime, fosters reconciliation, and promotes personal and collective transformation. This chapter has explored the philosophy, benefits, and practical applications of prioritizing healing over punishment, highlighting the potential of restorative justice to create a more compassionate and effective justice system. Subsequent chapters will delve deeper into other core values of restorative justice, providing further insights into its transformative impact.

Inclusive Dialogue: Encouraging Open Communication among Victims, Offenders, and Community Members

Inclusive dialogue is a core value of restorative justice, emphasizing the importance of open and respectful communication among all parties affected by a crime. This approach fosters understanding, empathy, and collaboration, paving the way for healing and reconciliation. In this chapter, we will explore the philosophy, benefits, and practical applications of inclusive dialogue in the context of restorative justice.

The Philosophy of Inclusive Dialogue

Understanding Inclusive Dialogue

Inclusive dialogue involves bringing together victims, offenders, and community members in a structured conversation to address the harm caused by crime. It focuses on ensuring that all voices are heard and respected, promoting a sense of shared responsibility and mutual understanding.

1. Participation of All Stakeholders: Inclusive dialogue ensures that victims, offenders, and community members are all given the opportunity to participate in the justice process.

2. Respectful Communication: The dialogue is conducted in a respectful manner, where each participant's perspective is valued and acknowledged.

3. Shared Understanding: Through open communication, participants gain a deeper understanding of the impact of the crime and the needs of those affected.

Theoretical Foundations

Inclusive dialogue is grounded in several theoretical principles that emphasize the importance of communication, empathy, and community involvement.

1. Communicative Action: Based on Jürgen Habermas's theory, communicative action involves dialogue aimed at reaching mutual understanding and consensus. This principle is central to restorative justice practices.

2. Relational Justice: Crime is seen as a violation of relationships. Inclusive dialogue aims to restore these relationships by fostering open communication and mutual respect.

3. Transformative Justice: The goal of inclusive dialogue is not only to address the harm caused by crime but also to transform the individuals and relationships involved, leading to personal and communal growth.

Benefits of Inclusive Dialogue

For Victims

1. Voice and Validation: Victims have the opportunity to share their experiences and feelings, which can be validating and empowering.

2. Emotional Healing: Expressing their emotions and receiving acknowledgment from the offender and the community can facilitate emotional healing for victims.

3. Sense of Justice: Inclusive dialogue allows victims to participate actively in the justice process, leading to a greater sense of justice and closure.

For Offenders

1. Accountability and Understanding: Offenders gain a deeper understanding of the impact of their actions, promoting accountability and remorse.

2. Opportunity for Apology: Offenders have the chance to apologize directly to their victims, which can be a crucial step in their rehabilitation.

3. Personal Growth: Engaging in inclusive dialogue encourages offenders to reflect on their behavior and commit to positive change.

For Communities

1. Strengthened Social Bonds: Inclusive dialogue fosters community involvement and support, strengthening social bonds and promoting collective healing.

2. Enhanced Trust: By prioritizing open communication and fairness, inclusive dialogue builds trust in the justice system and among community members.

3. Community Resilience: Inclusive dialogue helps build community resilience by addressing the broader impact of crime and fostering a sense of solidarity and shared responsibility.

Practical Applications of Inclusive Dialogue

Victim-Offender Mediation

Victim-offender mediation is a restorative practice that exemplifies inclusive dialogue. It involves facilitated meetings between victims and offenders to discuss the impact of the crime and agree on steps to repair the harm.

1. Preparation: Both parties are prepared for the mediation process, ensuring they understand its goals and are willing to engage constructively.
2. Facilitated Dialogue: A trained mediator guides the conversation, helping to navigate difficult emotions and ensure that the dialogue remains respectful and productive.
3. Agreement on Reparation: The parties work together to reach an agreement on how to repair the harm, which may include restitution, community service, or other forms of reparation.

Family Group Conferencing

Family group conferencing involves the extended family and support networks of both the victim and the offender. This practice recognizes the role of family and community in the healing process.

1. Inclusion of Support Networks: Family members and supporters are actively involved in the process, providing emotional support and contributing to the resolution.

2. Collaborative Decision-Making: The group works together to develop a plan for repairing the harm and supporting the offender's reintegration.

3. Strengthening Family Bonds: The process helps to strengthen family and community bonds, promoting a sense of collective responsibility and support.

Community Conferencing

Community conferencing involves a broader group of community members who are affected by the crime. This practice aims to address the wider impact of crime on the community and to involve the community in the justice process.

1. Community Participation: Community members participate in the process, sharing their perspectives and contributing to the resolution.

2. Collective Healing: The process promotes collective healing by addressing the harm caused to the community and fostering a sense of solidarity.

3. Building Resilience: By involving the community in the justice process, restorative justice helps to build community resilience and cohesion.

Case Studies Illustrating Inclusive Dialogue

Case Study 1: Healing After Theft

In a case involving theft, the victim and offender participated in a restorative justice conference. The victim expressed the emotional impact of the theft, while the offender acknowledged their actions and apologized. Community members also shared their perspectives on the broader impact of the crime. The inclusive dialogue led to an agreement on restitution and community service, fostering healing and reconciliation.

Case Study 2: Reconciliation after Domestic Violence

A family affected by domestic violence engaged in restorative justice practices. Through facilitated dialogue, the victim shared their trauma, and the offender took responsibility for their actions. Family members provided support and contributed to developing a plan for the offender's rehabilitation. The process helped the family to heal and rebuild their relationships.

Case Study 3: Community Healing after Vandalism

In a community affected by vandalism, restorative justice conferencing brought together the offenders, victims, and community members. The inclusive dialogue helped to repair relationships within the community, with the offenders agreeing to repair the damage and participate in community service. This process strengthened community bonds and promoted a sense of collective responsibility.

Challenges and Solutions

Overcoming Resistance to Dialogue

1. Building Trust: Establishing trust among participants is crucial. Facilitators play a key role in creating a safe and respectful environment for dialogue.

2. Educating Stakeholders: Educating stakeholders about the benefits of inclusive dialogue can help overcome skepticism and resistance.

3. Providing Support: Ongoing support for victims, offenders, and community members is essential to ensure the success of restorative practices.

Ensuring Fairness and Equity

1. Addressing Power Imbalances: Facilitators must be trained to recognize and address power imbalances to ensure that all voices are heard and respected.

2. Maintaining Neutrality: Facilitators must remain neutral and impartial, focusing on the needs and well-being of all participants.

3. Inclusive Practices: Restorative justice practices should be inclusive, ensuring that all affected parties have an opportunity to participate meaningfully.

Conclusion

Inclusive dialogue is a foundational value of restorative justice that prioritizes open and respectful communication among victims, offenders, and community members. By fostering understanding, empathy, and collaboration, inclusive dialogue promotes healing, accountability, and reconciliation. This chapter has explored the philosophy, benefits, and practical applications of inclusive dialogue, highlighting its potential to create a more just and compassionate society. Subsequent chapters will delve deeper into other core values of restorative justice, providing further insights into its transformative impact.

Core Values of Restorative Justice

Accountability and Responsibility: Offenders Taking Responsibility for Their Actions and Making Amends

Accountability and responsibility are central tenets of restorative justice. This approach emphasizes that offenders must acknowledge their wrongdoing, understand the impact of their actions, and take concrete steps to make amends. This chapter explores the philosophical, psychological, and practical aspects of accountability and responsibility in restorative justice.

The Philosophy of Accountability and Responsibility

Understanding Accountability

Accountability in restorative justice means that offenders must answer for their actions and face the people they have harmed. It involves a clear acknowledgment of wrongdoing and a commitment to make things right.

1. Acknowledgment of Harm: Offenders must recognize and admit the harm they have caused to victims and the community.

2. Personal Responsibility: Taking responsibility means accepting the consequences of one's actions and committing to change.

3. Making Amends: Offenders are expected to take steps to repair the harm, which can include apologies, restitution, and community service.

Theoretical Foundations

Accountability and responsibility are rooted in several theoretical principles that emphasize ethical behavior, personal growth, and social harmony.

1. Ethical Responsibility: Philosophers like Immanuel Kant have emphasized the importance of ethical responsibility, which involves acting in ways that respect the dignity and rights of others.

2. Moral Development: Psychologists such as Lawrence Kohlberg have explored stages of moral development, highlighting the importance of taking responsibility for one's actions as a sign of moral maturity.

3. Social Contract: The concept of the social contract, articulated by thinkers like Jean-Jacques Rousseau, underscores the idea that individuals have responsibilities to each other and to the community.

Benefits of Accountability and Responsibility

For Offenders

1. Personal Growth: Taking responsibility for their actions helps offenders develop a deeper understanding of the impact of their behavior and fosters personal growth.

2. Empathy and Remorse: Facing the people they have harmed can evoke empathy and remorse, which are crucial for genuine rehabilitation.

3. Rehabilitation: Accountability is a key component of rehabilitation, as it encourages offenders to make positive changes in their lives and reduces the likelihood of reoffending.

For Victims

1. Validation: When offenders take responsibility, it validates the victims' experiences and acknowledges the harm they have suffered.

2. Sense of Justice: Seeing offenders held accountable can provide victims with a sense of justice and closure.

3. Restoration of Trust: Accountability can help restore trust between victims and offenders, paving the way for reconciliation and healing.

For Communities

1. Community Safety: Holding offenders accountable contributes to community safety by addressing the root causes of criminal behavior and promoting rehabilitation.

2. Social Harmony: Accountability fosters social harmony by ensuring that offenders take responsibility for their actions and work to make amends.

3. Collective Responsibility: The process encourages a sense of collective responsibility, where the community supports both victims and offenders in the healing process.

Practical Applications of Accountability and Responsibility

Victim-Offender Mediation

Victim-offender mediation is a restorative practice that emphasizes accountability and responsibility. It involves facilitated meetings where offenders face their victims and take responsibility for their actions.

1. Preparation: Both parties are prepared for the mediation process, ensuring they understand its goals and are willing to engage constructively.

2. Facilitated Dialogue: A trained mediator guides the conversation, helping to navigate difficult emotions and ensure that the dialogue remains productive.

3. Agreement on Reparation: The parties work together to reach an agreement on how to repair the harm, which may include restitution, community service, or other forms of reparation.

Family Group Conferencing

Family group conferencing involves the extended family and support networks of both the victim and the offender. This practice emphasizes collective responsibility and support.

1. Family Involvement: Family members and supporters are actively involved in the process, providing emotional support and contributing to the resolution.

2. Collaborative Decision-Making: The group works together to develop a plan for repairing the harm and supporting the offender's reintegration.

3. Strengthening Family Bonds: The process helps to strengthen family and community bonds, promoting a sense of collective responsibility and support.

Community Conferencing

Community conferencing involves a broader group of community members who are affected by the crime. This practice emphasizes the role of the community in holding offenders accountable and supporting their rehabilitation.

1. Community Participation: Community members participate in the process, sharing their perspectives and contributing to the resolution.

2. Collective Healing: The process promotes collective healing by addressing the harm caused to the community and fostering a sense of solidarity.

3. Building Resilience: By involving the community in the justice process, restorative justice helps to build community resilience and cohesion.

Case Studies Illustrating Accountability and Responsibility

Case Study 1: Acknowledging Theft

In a case involving theft, the offender participated in a restorative justice conference with the victim and community members. The offender acknowledged the harm caused, apologized to the victim, and agreed to make restitution. The process fostered empathy and remorse in the offender, leading to personal growth and a commitment to change.

Case Study 2: Taking Responsibility for Domestic Violence

A family affected by domestic violence engaged in restorative justice practices. Through facilitated dialogue, the offender took responsibility for their actions and committed to change. The process included a plan for rehabilitation and ongoing support, helping the family to heal and rebuild their relationships.

Case Study 3: Community Accountability after Vandalism

In a community affected by vandalism, restorative justice conferencing brought together the offenders, victims, and community members. The offenders took responsibility for their actions, apologized, and agreed to repair the damage. This process strengthened community bonds and promoted a sense of collective responsibility.

Challenges and Solutions

Overcoming Denial and Resistance

1. Building Trust: Establishing trust among participants is crucial. Facilitators play a key role in creating a safe and respectful environment for dialogue.

2. Educating Offenders: Educating offenders about the benefits of taking responsibility can help overcome denial and resistance.

3. Providing Support: Ongoing support for victims, offenders, and community members is essential to ensure the success of restorative practices.

Ensuring Fairness and Equity

1. Addressing Power Imbalances: Facilitators must be trained to recognize and address power imbalances to ensure that all voices are heard and respected.

2. Maintaining Neutrality: Facilitators must remain neutral and impartial, focusing on the needs and well-being of all participants.

3. Inclusive Practices: Restorative justice practices should be inclusive, ensuring that all affected parties have an opportunity to participate meaningfully.

Conclusion

Accountability and responsibility are foundational values of restorative justice that emphasize the importance of offenders taking responsibility for their actions and making amends. By fostering a sense of accountability, restorative justice promotes personal growth, rehabilitation, and healing for offenders, while providing validation, a sense of justice, and restoration for victims. This chapter has explored the philosophical, psychological, and practical aspects of accountability and responsibility, highlighting their potential to create a more just and compassionate society. Subsequent chapters will delve deeper into other core values of restorative justice, providing further insights into its transformative impact.

Community Involvement: Engaging the Community in the Justice Process to Foster Collective Healing and Support

Community involvement is a core value of restorative justice, emphasizing the active engagement of the community in the justice process. By involving the community, restorative justice fosters collective healing, promotes social cohesion, and supports both victims and offenders in their journey toward restoration. This chapter explores the philosophy, benefits, and practical applications of community involvement in restorative justice.

The Philosophy of Community Involvement

Understanding Community Involvement

Community involvement in restorative justice refers to the active participation of community members in addressing the harm caused by crime and supporting the healing process. This approach recognizes that crime affects not only the direct victims but also the wider community.

1. Collective Responsibility: Community involvement promotes a sense of collective responsibility, where

community members work together to address the harm and support those affected.

2. Social Cohesion: Engaging the community in the justice process helps to strengthen social bonds and promote a sense of belonging and mutual support.

3. Restorative Communities: By involving the community, restorative justice aims to create restorative communities where individuals are supported, harm is addressed, and relationships are restored.

Theoretical Foundations

Community involvement is grounded in several theoretical principles that emphasize the importance of social connections, mutual support, and collective well-being.

1. Communitarianism: This philosophy emphasizes the importance of community and social bonds in achieving individual and collective well-being.

2. Social Capital: Sociologist Robert Putnam's concept of social capital highlights the value of social networks, trust, and reciprocity in fostering strong communities.

3. Collective Efficacy: The idea of collective efficacy, proposed by Robert Sampson, emphasizes the community's ability to work together to achieve common goals, including addressing crime and promoting safety.

Benefits of Community Involvement

For Victims

1. Support and Validation: Community involvement provides victims with a network of support and validation, helping them to feel understood and cared for.

2. Restored Sense of Safety: Engaging the community in the justice process can help restore a sense of safety and security for victims.

3. Community Healing: When the community actively participates in addressing harm, it fosters a sense of communal healing and solidarity.

For Offenders

1. Reintegration Support: Community involvement helps to support the reintegration of offenders, providing them with the resources and encouragement needed to make positive changes.

2. Accountability: Offenders are held accountable not only to their victims but also to the community, reinforcing the importance of taking responsibility for their actions.

3. Personal Growth: Through community involvement, offenders have the opportunity to engage in positive social interactions and contribute to the community, fostering personal growth and development.

For Communities

1. Strengthened Social Bonds: Community involvement in restorative justice helps to strengthen social bonds, promoting trust, cooperation, and mutual support.

2. Increased Social Cohesion: By working together to address crime and support those affected, communities become more cohesive and resilient.

3. Collective Healing: Engaging the community in the justice process promotes collective healing, addressing the broader impact of crime and fostering a sense of solidarity.

Practical Applications of Community Involvement

Community Conferencing

Community conferencing involves bringing together victims, offenders, and community members to discuss the impact of the crime and develop a plan for repairing the harm.

1. Inclusive Participation: Community members are actively involved in the process, sharing their perspectives and contributing to the resolution.

2. Facilitated Dialogue: A trained facilitator guides the conversation, ensuring that all voices are heard and respected.

3. Collective Decision-Making: The group works together to develop a plan for repairing the harm and supporting the offender's reintegration.

Restorative Circles

Restorative circles are a practice that involves community members in a structured dialogue to address harm and promote healing.

1. Circle Format: Participants sit in a circle, promoting equality and open communication.

2. Talking Piece: A talking piece is used to ensure that everyone has an opportunity to speak and be heard.

3. Shared Responsibility: The circle process emphasizes shared responsibility for addressing harm and supporting those affected.

Community Service

Community service is a form of reparation that involves offenders contributing to the community as a way of making amends for their actions.

1. Meaningful Contributions: Offenders engage in activities that benefit the community, such as cleaning up public spaces, helping with community projects, or providing assistance to those in need.

2. Building Positive Relationships: Through community service, offenders build positive relationships with community members, fostering trust and mutual respect.

3. Reintegration: Community service helps to support the reintegration of offenders by providing them with opportunities to contribute positively to the community.

Case Studies Illustrating Community Involvement

Case Study 1: Community Healing After Vandalism

In a community affected by vandalism, restorative justice conferencing brings together the offenders, victims, and community members. The inclusive dialogue helped to repair relationships within the community, with the offenders agreeing to repair the damage and participate in community service. This process strengthened community bonds and promoted a sense of collective responsibility.

Case Study 2: Support for Domestic Violence Survivors

A community-based restorative justice program provided support for survivors of domestic violence. Through restorative circles, survivors were able to share their experiences and receive validation and support from the community. Offenders participated in community service and received ongoing support for rehabilitation. This approach fostered healing for survivors and promoted the reintegration of offenders.

Case Study 3: Reintegration after Theft

In a case involving theft, the offender participated in a community conferencing process with the victim and community members. The offender acknowledged the harm caused and committed to making restitution. Community members provided support and resources to help the offender reintegrate and make positive changes. This process promoted healing for the victim and supported the offender's rehabilitation.

Challenges and Solutions

Overcoming Resistance to Community Involvement

1. Building Trust: Establishing trust among participants is crucial. Facilitators play a key role in creating a safe and respectful environment for dialogue.

2. Educating the Community: Educating community members about the benefits of restorative justice and their role in the process can help overcome resistance.

3. Providing Support: Ongoing support for victims, offenders, and community members is essential to ensure the success of restorative practices.

Ensuring Inclusive Participation

1. Addressing Power Imbalances: Facilitators must be trained to recognize and address power imbalances to ensure that all voices are heard and respected.

2. Maintaining Neutrality: Facilitators must remain neutral and impartial, focusing on the needs and well-being of all participants.

3. Inclusive Practices: Restorative justice practices should be inclusive, ensuring that all affected parties have an opportunity to participate meaningfully.

Conclusion

Community involvement is a foundational value of restorative justice that emphasizes the active engagement of the community in the justice process. By fostering collective healing, promoting social cohesion, and supporting both victims and offenders, community involvement helps to create restorative communities where individuals are supported, harm is addressed, and relationships are restored. This chapter has explored the philosophy, benefits, and practical applications of community involvement in restorative justice, highlighting its potential to create a more just and compassionate society. Subsequent chapters will delve deeper into other core values of restorative justice, providing further insights into its transformative impact.

Ethical Considerations

Restorative justice operates on principles of respect, dignity, and empathy. These ethical foundations ensure that all participants are treated fairly and with compassion throughout the restorative justice process. This chapter delves into the ethical frameworks that guide restorative justice practices, exploring the principles of respect, dignity, empathy, fairness, and equity.

Principles of Respect

Understanding Respect

Respect in restorative justice means acknowledging and valuing the inherent worth of each individual involved in the process, regardless of their role as victim, offender, or community member.

1. Acknowledgment of Humanity: All participants are recognized as individuals with inherent worth and dignity.

2. Non-Judgmental Attitude: Respect involves approaching each participant without judgment, recognizing that everyone is capable of growth and change.

3. Active Listening: Respectful communication includes actively listening to each participant's perspective and validating their experiences.

Practical Applications of Respect

1. Victim-Centered Approach: Ensuring that victims feel heard, valued, and supported throughout the restorative justice process.

2. Offender Accountability: Encouraging offenders to take responsibility for their actions in a respectful and non-shaming manner.

3. Community Involvement: Valuing the contributions and perspectives of community members in the restorative process.

Principles of Dignity

Understanding Dignity

Dignity in restorative justice involves treating all participants with honor and respect, and recognizing their intrinsic value as human beings.

1. Intrinsic Worth: Acknowledging that every person has intrinsic worth and deserves to be treated with honor and respect.

2. Respectful Treatment: Ensuring that all interactions are conducted with respect, avoiding any form of humiliation or degradation.

3. Empowerment: Empowering participants to express their feelings, needs, and perspectives, thereby affirming their dignity.

Practical Applications of Dignity

1. Facilitated Dialogue: Conducting restorative justice dialogues in a manner that upholds the dignity of all participants.

2. Supportive Environment: Creating a supportive environment where participants feel safe and respected.

3. Restorative Outcomes: Ensuring that the outcomes of the restorative process uphold the dignity of all parties involved.

Principles of Empathy

Understanding Empathy

Empathy in restorative justice means understanding and sharing the feelings of others, fostering a sense of connection and compassion among participants.

1. Emotional Connection: Developing an emotional connection with participants by understanding their experiences and feelings.

2. Compassionate Response: Responding to participants with compassion and understanding, recognizing their pain and suffering.

3. Mutual Understanding: Fostering mutual understanding and empathy among victims, offenders, and community members.

Practical Applications of Empathy

1. Victim Support: Providing empathetic support to victims, acknowledging their pain, and validating their experiences.

2. Offender Rehabilitation: Encouraging offenders to develop empathy for their victims and understand the impact of their actions.

3. Community Healing: Promoting empathy and understanding within the community, fostering collective healing and support.

Principles of Fairness and Equity

Understanding Fairness and Equity

Fairness and equity in restorative justice involve ensuring that all participants are treated justly and that the process is inclusive and impartial.

1. Impartial Process: Conducting the restorative justice process in an impartial manner, without favoritism or bias.

2. Inclusive Participation: Ensuring that all affected parties have an equal opportunity to participate and be heard.

3. Equitable Outcomes: Striving for outcomes that are fair and equitable for all participants, addressing their needs and concerns.

Practical Applications of Fairness and Equity

1. Facilitator Neutrality: Ensuring that facilitators remain neutral and impartial, focusing on the needs and well-being of all participants.

2. Addressing Power Imbalances: Recognizing and addressing power imbalances to ensure that all voices are heard and respected.

3. Inclusive Practices: Implementing inclusive practices that ensure equal participation and consideration for all affected parties.

Ethical Frameworks Guiding Restorative Justice

Restorative Ethics

Restorative ethics is a framework that guides restorative justice practices, emphasizing principles of respect, dignity, empathy, fairness, and equity.

1. Respect for Persons: Upholding the respect and dignity of all participants, recognizing their inherent worth and value.

2. Commitment to Justice: Ensuring that the restorative justice process is conducted fairly and equitably, with a commitment to justice for all parties.

3. Compassionate Engagement: Engaging with participants compassionately, fostering empathy and understanding throughout the process.

Human Rights Framework

Restorative justice aligns with a human rights framework, ensuring that the rights and dignity of all participants are upheld.

1. Right to Dignity: Recognizing and upholding the right to dignity for all participants, ensuring respectful and humane treatment.

2. Right to Participation: Ensuring that all affected parties have the right to participate in the restorative justice process.

3. Right to Fair Treatment: Guaranteeing fair treatment for all participants, addressing their needs and concerns in an equitable manner.

Case Studies Illustrating Ethical Considerations

Case Study 1: Respecting Victim Dignity

In a case involving assault, the restorative justice process ensured that the victim's dignity was upheld throughout. The victim was provided with a safe and supportive environment to share their experiences, and their needs were prioritized in the resolution process. The offender acknowledged the harm caused and took steps to make amends, promoting healing and respect for the victim's dignity.

Case Study 2: Empathy in Action

A community affected by a series of burglaries engaged in a restorative justice process that emphasized empathy. Offenders participated in facilitated dialogues with victims, where they developed a deeper understanding of the impact of their actions. Through these interactions, offenders expressed genuine remorse and committed to making amends, fostering mutual empathy and healing.

Case Study 3: Ensuring Fairness and Equity

In the case of vandalism, the restorative justice process focused on ensuring fairness and equity. All affected parties, including victims, offenders, and community members, were given an equal opportunity to participate and share their perspectives. The facilitator maintained neutrality, and the process addressed power imbalances to ensure that all voices were heard. The outcome was a fair and equitable resolution that met the needs of all participants.

Challenges and Solutions

Overcoming Ethical Challenges

1. Building Trust: Establishing trust among participants is crucial. Facilitators play a key role in creating a safe and respectful environment for dialogue.

2. Maintaining Neutrality: Ensuring that facilitators remain neutral and impartial, focusing on the needs and well-being of all participants.

3. Providing Support: Ongoing support for victims, offenders, and community members is essential to uphold ethical principles and ensure the success of restorative practices.

Ensuring Ethical Practices

1. Training Facilitators: Providing comprehensive training for facilitators to ensure they understand and uphold the ethical principles of restorative justice

2. Implementing Guidelines: Establishing clear guidelines and protocols for the restorative justice process to ensure ethical practices are maintained.

3. Monitoring and Evaluation: Regularly monitoring and evaluating the restorative justice process to ensure that ethical standards are upheld and that participants are treated fairly and with compassion.

Conclusion

Ethical considerations are foundational to restorative justice, guiding the practice through principles of respect, dignity, empathy, fairness, and equity. By upholding these principles, restorative justice ensures that all participants are treated fairly and with compassion, fostering healing, accountability, and reconciliation. This chapter has explored the ethical frameworks that guide restorative justice practices, highlighting their importance in creating a just and compassionate society. Subsequent chapters will delve deeper into other core values of restorative justice, providing further insights into its transformative impact.

CHAPTER 03

HISTORY AND DEVELOPMENT OF RESTORATIVE JUSTICE

Origins of Restorative Justice

Restorative justice has deep roots in indigenous practices and community-based justice systems. These early forms of justice focused on healing and restoring relationships rather than punishment. This chapter traces the historical evolution of restorative justice, from ancient traditions to its modern adoption in various legal systems worldwide.

Ancient Indigenous Practices

Native American Traditions

Among many Native American tribes, justice was a communal process aimed at restoring harmony within the community. Practices varied among tribes, but common elements included:

1. Peacemaking Circles: These circles involve the community in a dialogue process to resolve conflicts and heal relationships. Participants sat in a circle, promoting equality and open communication.

2. Elders' Role: Elders played a crucial role in guiding the process, using their wisdom to facilitate dialogue and mediate disputes.

3. Focus on Healing: The primary goal was to heal the harm caused by the offense, restore relationships, and reintegrate the offender into the community.

Maori Practices in New Zealand

The Maori of New Zealand practiced a form of restorative justice known as "whakawhanaungatanga," which emphasized the importance of relationships and community.

1. Whanau Involvement: The extended family (whanau) was involved in addressing the harm and supporting the healing process.

2. Hui Meetings: These meetings involved open dialogue, where all parties could speak and be heard. The goal was to reach a consensus on how to repair the harm.

3. Restorative Actions: Offenders were expected to take actions to make amends, such as offering apologies, providing restitution, or performing community service.

African Traditions

In many African cultures, restorative justice practices were embedded in community life and aimed at maintaining social harmony.

1. Ubuntu Philosophy: The concept of "ubuntu" emphasizes interconnectedness and mutual respect. Justice practices reflected this philosophy by focusing on reconciliation and community cohesion.

2. Community Councils: Disputes were often resolved through community councils, where elders and community members discussed the issue and sought a resolution that restored harmony.

3. Restitution and Reconciliation: Offenders were encouraged to make restitution and seek reconciliation with those they had harmed, reinforcing the community's values and relationships.

Historical Evolution

Middle Ages in Europe

During the Middle Ages, European societies also practiced forms of restorative justice. Before the rise of centralized state justice systems, local communities handled disputes through various means.

1. Manorial Courts: In feudal societies, manorial courts addressed minor offenses through mediation and restitution rather than punishment.

2. Tithing System: In England, the tithing system required groups of ten households to be collectively responsible for each other's behavior, promoting community accountability and support.

3. Reparative Practices: Many European communities emphasized reparative justice, where offenders were required to compensate victims for their losses and repair the harm.

Colonial Influences and Decline

With the advent of colonialism and the spread of European legal systems, many indigenous and community-based justice practices were suppressed or marginalized.

1. Imposition of Western Legal Systems: Colonial powers imposed their legal systems on indigenous populations, often disregarding and undermining traditional justice practices.

2. Criminalization and Punishment: The focus shifted to criminalization and punishment, with an emphasis on state authority and retributive justice.

3. Erosion of Community Practices: As centralized state justice systems took hold, community-based practices declined, leading to a loss of restorative justice traditions.

Revival and Modern Adoption

20th Century Resurgence

The modern resurgence of restorative justice began in the latter half of the 20th century, as scholars, activists, and practitioners sought alternatives to punitive justice systems.

1. Pioneering Programs: Early restorative justice programs emerged in North America and Europe, focusing on victim-offender mediation and family group conferencing.

2. Research and Advocacy: Researchers and advocates highlighted the limitations of retributive justice and promoted restorative practices as more effective and humane alternatives.

3. Institutional Support: Governments and institutions began to support restorative justice initiatives, incorporating them into juvenile justice systems, schools, and community programs.

Global Adoption

Restorative justice has since been adopted in various forms around the world, reflecting diverse cultural and legal contexts.

1. Legislative Frameworks: Many countries have introduced legislation to support restorative justice practices, recognizing their benefits for victims, offenders, and communities.

2. Integration into Legal Systems: Restorative justice has been integrated into formal legal systems as an alternative or complement to traditional punitive measures.

3. International Influence: Organizations such as the United Nations and the European Union have endorsed restorative justice, promoting its principles and practices globally.

Case Studies of Historical Practices

Case Study 1: The Navajo Peacemaking System

The Navajo Nation has maintained its traditional peacemaking system, which emphasizes healing and reconciliation.

1. Peacemaking Process: The process involves community members, including the victim, offender, and their families, in a dialogue facilitated by a peacemaker.

2. Focus on Relationships: The goal is to restore harmony by addressing the underlying causes of the conflict and repairing relationships.

3. Cultural Continuity: The Navajo peacemaking system reflects the community's cultural values and traditions, ensuring its relevance and effectiveness.

Case Study 2: The Maori Family Group Conferencing

New Zealand's adoption of family group conferencing (FGC) is rooted in Maori traditions and has been integrated into the juvenile justice system.

1. Involvement of Whanau: FGC involves the extended family in decision-making, ensuring that the victim, offender, and their families are all part of the process.

2. Consensus Building: The process aims to reach a consensus on how to address the harm and support the offender's rehabilitation.

3. Successful Outcomes: Research has shown that FGC reduces recidivism and promotes positive outcomes for both victims and offenders.

Conclusion

The origins of restorative justice are deeply rooted in indigenous practices and community-based justice systems that emphasize healing, reconciliation, and the restoration of relationships. Despite the decline of these practices with the rise of centralized state justice systems, restorative justice has experienced a resurgence in the 20th century and has been adopted in various forms around the world. By drawing on the wisdom of traditional practices and integrating them into modern legal systems, restorative justice offers a humane and effective alternative to punitive approaches, fostering healing and transformation for individuals and communities alike. Subsequent chapters will explore the principles, practices, and impacts of restorative justice in greater detail, providing further insights into its transformative potential.

Milestones in Restorative Justice

Early Indigenous Practices: Exploring the Justice Practices of Native American, Maori, and Other Indigenous Cultures

Restorative justice has deep roots in the traditions of indigenous cultures around the world. These cultures have long practiced forms of justice that emphasize healing, reconciliation, and the restoration of relationships rather than punitive measures. This chapter explores the justice practices of Native American, Maori, and other indigenous cultures, highlighting how their approaches to justice have influenced modern restorative justice.

Native American Justice Practices

Peacemaking Circles

One of the most well-known Native American justice practices is the use of peacemaking circles. These circles involve community members in a dialogue process to resolve conflicts and heal relationships.

1. Structure and Process: Peacemaking circles typically include the victim, the offender, their families, and community members. A respected elder or peacemaker facilitates the circle, guiding the discussion and ensuring that everyone has an opportunity to speak.
2. Healing Focus: The primary goal of peacemaking circles is to heal the harm caused by the offense. This involves acknowledging the impact of the crime, expressing emotions, and finding a way to move forward together.
3. Community Responsibility: The circle format emphasizes the collective responsibility of the community to support both the victim and the offender in the healing process.

Role of Elders

In many Native American cultures, elders play a crucial role in the justice process. Their wisdom and experience are valued in resolving conflicts and guiding the community toward healing.

1. Mediation and Guidance: Elders often serve as mediators, helping to facilitate discussions and provide guidance to those involved in the conflict.

2. Cultural Knowledge: Elders bring a deep understanding of cultural values and traditions, which helps to ground the justice process in the community's unique context.

3. Mentorship: By mentoring younger community members, elders help to reinforce the principles of restorative justice and ensure that these practices are passed down through generations.

Navajo Peacemaking

The Navajo Nation's peacemaking system is a notable example of indigenous restorative justice. It emphasizes restoring harmony and healing relationships within the community.

1. K'é Principle: Central to Navajo peacemaking is the concept of K'é, which refers to kinship and the interconnectedness of all people. This principle guides the process of reconciliation and healing.

2. Inclusive Process: Peacemaking involves the participation of all affected parties, including the victim, the offender, their families, and community members.

3. Focus on Restoration: The goal is to restore balance and harmony by addressing the underlying causes of the conflict and ensuring that the offender takes responsibility for their actions.

Maori Justice Practices

Whakawhanaungatanga

The Maori concept of whakawhanaungatanga emphasizes the importance of relationships and community in the justice process.

1. Family Group Conferencing (FGC): This practice involves the extended family (whanau) in addressing the harm and supporting the healing process. FGC has been widely adopted in New Zealand's juvenile justice system.

2. Consensus Building: The goal of FGC is to reach a consensus on how to address the harm and support the offender's rehabilitation. This often involves open dialogue and collaborative decision-making.

3. Restorative Actions: Offenders are encouraged to take actions to make amends, such as offering apologies, providing restitution, or performing community service.

Hui Meetings

Hui meetings are traditional Maori gatherings used to resolve conflicts and make important decisions.

1. Inclusivity: Hui meetings involve all affected parties, including victims, offenders, their families, and community leaders. This ensures that everyone's voice is heard and respected.

2. Cultural Rituals: These meetings often include cultural rituals and protocols that reinforce the values of respect, connection, and community.

3. Restorative Focus: The aim is to repair relationships, restore harmony, and ensure that the offender takes responsibility for their actions.

Maori Values

Maori justice practices are deeply rooted in cultural values that emphasize community, respect, and restoration.

1. Mana: The concept of mana refers to the inherent dignity and respect of individuals. Restorative justice practices aim to uphold and restore mana for both victims and offenders.

2. Tapu and Noa: Tapu refers to the sacredness and restrictions associated with certain actions or individuals, while noa refers to the state of normalcy and balance. Justice practices often aim to restore balance by addressing violations of tapu.

3. Aroha: The value of aroha, or love and compassion, guides the justice process, ensuring that all actions are taken with empathy and care.

African Justice Practices

Ubuntu Philosophy

In many African cultures, the philosophy of ubuntu emphasizes interconnectedness and mutual respect, guiding justice practices that focus on reconciliation and community cohesion.

1. Interconnectedness: Ubuntu recognizes that individuals are interconnected and that harm to one person affects the entire community. Justice practices aim to restore these connections.

2. Reconciliation: The primary goal is reconciliation and the restoration of harmony within the community. This involves addressing the harm and ensuring that the offender takes responsibility for their actions.

3. Community Councils: Disputes are often resolved through community councils, where elders and community members discuss the issue and seek a resolution that restores harmony.

Traditional Courts

In various African cultures, traditional courts have long practiced forms of restorative justice that emphasize mediation, restitution, and reconciliation.

1. Role of Elders: Elders play a central role in traditional courts, using their wisdom and experience to mediate disputes and guide the community toward resolution.

2. Focus on Restoration: The aim is to restore relationships and ensure that offenders make amends for their actions, often through restitution or community service.

3. Cultural Rituals: Traditional courts often incorporate cultural rituals and practices that reinforce community values and promote healing.

Conclusion

The justice practices of indigenous cultures around the world have long emphasized healing, reconciliation, and the restoration of relationships. These early forms of restorative justice have influenced modern restorative justice practices, offering valuable insights into how communities can address harm in a way that promotes healing and social cohesion. By drawing on the wisdom of these traditional practices, modern restorative justice seeks to create a more humane and effective justice system that prioritizes the well-being of individuals and communities. Subsequent chapters will explore the development and implementation of restorative justice in various contexts, providing further insights into its transformative potential.

20th Century Revival: The Resurgence of Restorative Justice in the 1970s and 1980s

The modern revival of restorative justice in the 20th century marked a significant shift in the way societies approached crime and justice. Emerging in the 1970s and 1980s, this resurgence was driven by dissatisfaction with the punitive nature of traditional justice systems and a growing recognition of the benefits of restorative approaches. This chapter explores the key developments, influential figures, and foundational programs that contributed to the revival of restorative justice during this period.

Dissatisfaction with Traditional Justice Systems

Rising Criticism

In the mid-20th century, there was increasing criticism of traditional justice systems, particularly their emphasis on punishment and incarceration.

1. High Recidivism Rates: Traditional justice systems were often ineffective in preventing reoffending, leading to high recidivism rates and overcrowded prisons.

2. Victim Marginalization: Victims were frequently marginalized in the justice process, with their needs and voices often overlooked.

3. Community Disconnection: Punitive justice systems tended to disconnect offenders from their communities, hindering reintegration and rehabilitation.

Search for Alternatives

The search for more effective and humane alternatives to punitive justice systems led to renewed interest in restorative justice principles.

1. Community-Based Approaches: There was a growing recognition of the value of community-based approaches that involved victims, offenders, and community members in the justice process.

2. Focus on Healing: The emphasis on healing and restoration rather than punishment resonated with advocates seeking to address the root causes of crime and support victims.

3. Holistic Justice: Restorative justice offered a more holistic approach that aimed to repair harm, restore relationships, and promote social harmony.

Key Developments in the 1970s

Victim-Offender Reconciliation Programs (VORP)

One of the foundational developments in the revival of restorative justice was the establishment of Victim-Offender Reconciliation Programs (VORP).

1. Origin: The first VORP was initiated in 1974 in Kitchener, Ontario, Canada, by Mennonite Central Committee members Mark Yantzi and Dave Worth. The program was inspired by the principles of restorative justice

and aimed to bring victims and offenders together for dialogue and reconciliation.

2. Process: VORP facilitated meetings between victims and offenders, where they could discuss the impact of the crime, express their feelings, and negotiate a plan for restitution and reparation.

3. Impact: The success of the Kitchener VORP led to the establishment of similar programs across North America and Europe, demonstrating the effectiveness of restorative justice in addressing harm and promoting healing.

Family Group Conferencing (FGC)

Another significant development in the 1970s was the introduction of Family Group Conferencing (FGC) in New Zealand.

1. Maori Influence: FGC was influenced by Maori traditions of communal decision-making and the importance of family (whanau) in addressing harm and supporting rehabilitation.

2. Juvenile Justice: The New Zealand juvenile justice system adopted FGC as a way to involve the family and community in the justice process, particularly for young offenders.

3. Collaborative Approach: FGC involved the victim, the offender, their families, and community members in a

facilitated meeting to discuss the impact of the crime and develop a plan for reparation and support.

Influential Figures in the Revival of Restorative Justice

Howard Zehr

Howard Zehr is often referred to as the "grandfather" of restorative justice for his pioneering work in the field.

1. Key Contributions: Zehr's book, "Changing Lenses: A New Focus for Crime and Justice" (1990), provided a comprehensive framework for understanding restorative justice and its principles.

2. Educational Impact: Zehr's work has been instrumental in educating practitioners, policymakers, and the public about restorative justice, influencing the development of programs and policies worldwide.

3. Philosophical Foundations: Zehr emphasized the importance of viewing crime as a violation of people and relationships rather than merely a violation of the law, advocating for a justice system focused on healing and restoration.

John Braithwaite

John Braithwaite, an Australian criminologist, made significant contributions to the theoretical foundations of restorative justice.

1. Reintegrative Shaming: Braithwaite's concept of reintegrative shaming highlights the importance of condemning the crime while supporting the offender's reintegration into society.

2. Community Focus: Braithwaite's work emphasized the role of the community in the justice process, advocating for practices that promote social cohesion and collective responsibility.

3. Global Influence: Braithwaite's research and writings have influenced restorative justice practices and policies in various countries, contributing to its global adoption.

Foundational Programs and Models

Circles of Support and Accountability (COSA)

Circles of Support and Accountability (COSA) emerged as a restorative justice model focused on supporting high-risk offenders upon their release from prison.

1. Community Involvement: COSA involves a circle of community volunteers who provide support, accountability, and guidance to the offender, helping them reintegrate into society.

2. Restorative Focus: The program emphasizes the importance of building relationships, addressing harm, and promoting positive change.

3. Effectiveness: Research has shown that COSA significantly reduces recidivism rates among high-risk offenders, demonstrating the effectiveness of community-based restorative justice approaches.

Restorative Circles

Restorative circles, inspired by indigenous practices, became a foundational model in the modern revival of restorative justice.

1. Circle Format: Participants sit in a circle, promoting equality and open communication. A talking piece is used to ensure that everyone has an opportunity to speak.

2. Facilitated Dialogue: A trained facilitator guides the dialogue, helping participants address harm, express emotions, and develop a plan for reparation.

3. Community Healing: Restorative circles involve victims, offenders, and community members, fostering collective healing and social cohesion.

Institutional Support and Expansion

Government and Legal System Integration

In the 1980s, governments and legal systems began to integrate restorative justice practices into their frameworks.

1. Legislative Support: Countries such as Canada, New Zealand, and Australia introduced legislation to support

restorative justice programs, recognizing their benefits for victims, offenders, and communities.

2. Juvenile Justice Systems: Restorative justice practices were particularly embraced in juvenile justice systems, where they were seen as more effective and humane alternatives to punitive measures.

3. Pilot Programs: Many jurisdictions launched pilot programs to test the effectiveness of restorative justice, leading to broader adoption and institutional support.

International Influence

International organizations and networks played a crucial role in promoting and supporting the revival of restorative justice.

1. United Nations: The United Nations endorsed restorative justice principles and practices, encouraging member states to incorporate them into their justice systems.

2. European Union: The European Union supported restorative justice initiatives, providing funding and policy guidance to member countries.

3. Restorative Justice Networks: Networks and organizations such as the Restorative Justice Network and the European Forum for Restorative Justice facilitated collaboration, research, and advocacy, promoting the global spread of restorative justice.

Conclusion

The 20th-century revival of restorative justice in the 1970s and 1980s marked a significant shift towards more humane and effective approaches to justice. Driven by dissatisfaction with punitive justice systems and inspired by indigenous practices, this resurgence saw the development of foundational programs, influential theoretical contributions, and growing institutional support. By emphasizing healing, reconciliation, and community involvement, restorative justice has offered a transformative alternative that continues to evolve and expand worldwide. Subsequent chapters will explore the principles, practices, and impacts of restorative justice in greater detail, providing further insights into its transformative potential.

Global Adoption: How Restorative Justice Has Been Integrated into Legal Systems Across Different Countries

Restorative justice has gained international recognition and has been integrated into legal systems across various countries. This chapter explores how different nations have adopted and implemented restorative justice practices, the legislative frameworks supporting these practices, and the impact on their justice systems.

Overview of Global Adoption

Restorative Justice Principles

Restorative justice principles emphasize repairing harm, restoring relationships, and involving all stakeholders in the justice process. These principles have been embraced globally due to their effectiveness in addressing the needs of victims, offenders, and communities.

1. Repairing Harm: The focus is on repairing the harm caused by criminal behavior through dialogue, restitution, and community service.

2. Restoring Relationships: Restorative justice aims to restore relationships between victims, offenders, and the community.

3. Inclusive Participation: The process involves victims, offenders, and community members, ensuring that all voices are heard and respected.

North America

Canada

Canada has been a pioneer in adopting restorative justice practices, particularly within its juvenile justice system.

1. Legislative Framework: The Youth Criminal Justice Act (YCJA) of 2003 emphasizes the use of restorative justice approaches for young offenders, including victim-offender mediation and family group conferencing.

2. Community-Based Programs: Numerous community-based programs across Canada facilitate

restorative justice practices, supported by governmental and non-governmental organizations.

3. Impact on Recidivism: Studies have shown that restorative justice programs in Canada significantly reduce recidivism rates among young offenders, promoting rehabilitation and community reintegration.

United States

In the United States, restorative justice has been integrated into both juvenile and adult justice systems, with a focus on community-based initiatives.

1. Juvenile Justice: States like Colorado, Minnesota, and Vermont have incorporated restorative justice into their juvenile justice systems, emphasizing rehabilitation and restorative practices.

2. School-Based Programs: Many schools in the U.S. have adopted restorative justice practices to address disciplinary issues, reduce suspensions, and promote a positive school climate.

3. Community Restorative Justice: Community programs, such as Circles of Support and Accountability (COSA), support high-risk offenders' reintegration by providing community support and accountability.

Europe

United Kingdom

The United Kingdom has integrated restorative justice practices into its criminal justice system, supported by a robust legislative framework.

1. Legislation: The Crime and Courts Act 2013 and the Victims' Code of Practice emphasize the use of restorative justice in the criminal justice process.

2. Restorative Justice Councils: The UK has established Restorative Justice Councils to promote and support the implementation of restorative justice practices nationwide.

3. Police and Prisons: Restorative justice practices have been adopted by police forces and prisons, providing opportunities for offenders to make amends and for victims to participate in the justice process.

European Union

The European Union has endorsed restorative justice and encouraged its member states to integrate restorative practices into their justice systems.

1. Framework Decisions: The EU's Framework Decision on the standing of victims in criminal proceedings (2001) and the Victims' Rights Directive (2012) support the use of restorative justice.

2. Funding and Research: The EU provides funding for restorative justice projects and supports research to evaluate the effectiveness of these practices.

3. Cross-Border Collaboration: The European Forum for Restorative Justice facilitates collaboration and knowledge-sharing among EU member states, promoting the adoption of restorative justice.

Oceania

New Zealand

New Zealand is renowned for its pioneering use of restorative justice, particularly through the incorporation of Maori practices.

1. Family Group Conferencing (FGC): New Zealand's juvenile justice system mandates the use of FGC, which involves the offender's family in the justice process.

2. Legislative Support: The Children, Young Persons, and Their Families Act 1989 established the legal framework for restorative justice in New Zealand.

3. Cultural Integration: Restorative justice practices in New Zealand are deeply influenced by Maori cultural values, emphasizing community involvement and holistic healing.

Australia

Australia has widely adopted restorative justice practices, with significant developments in both juvenile and adult justice systems.

1. Juvenile Justice: States like New South Wales and Queensland have integrated restorative justice into their juvenile justice systems, using youth justice conferencing to address offenses.

2. Indigenous Practices: Australia's restorative justice practices often draw on Indigenous traditions, promoting culturally sensitive approaches to justice.

3. Community-Based Programs: Numerous community-based programs across Australia support restorative justice, offering mediation, conferencing, and circles to address harm and promote healing.

Asia

Japan

Japan has incorporated restorative justice principles into its legal system, focusing on mediation and reconciliation.

1. Victim-Offender Mediation: Japan's legal system promotes victim-offender mediation, providing opportunities for dialogue and reparation.

2. Community Involvement: Community-based programs facilitate restorative justice practices, emphasizing

the role of the community in supporting victims and offenders.

3. Cultural Context: Restorative justice practices in Japan are influenced by cultural values of harmony and reconciliation, aligning with traditional conflict resolution methods.

South Korea

South Korea has seen a growing interest in restorative justice, with initiatives supported by both the government and civil society.

1. Legislative Developments: Recent legal reforms have introduced restorative justice practices into the juvenile justice system, promoting rehabilitation and reintegration.

2. Pilot Programs: Pilot programs in schools and communities are testing the effectiveness of restorative justice, with promising results in reducing recidivism and promoting healing.

3. Research and Advocacy: Academic institutions and NGOs in South Korea are actively researching and advocating for restorative justice, contributing to its broader adoption.

Africa

South Africa

South Africa's adoption of restorative justice has been influenced by its post-apartheid commitment to reconciliation and healing.

1. Truth and Reconciliation Commission (TRC): The TRC, established in 1995, is a notable example of restorative justice in practice, focusing on truth-telling, accountability, and reconciliation.

2. Legislative Framework: South Africa's legal system incorporates restorative justice principles, particularly in juvenile justice and community courts.

3. Community Programs: Community-based restorative justice programs address a range of issues, from domestic violence to property crimes, promoting reconciliation and social cohesion.

Uganda

Uganda has integrated restorative justice into its traditional justice systems, particularly through the use of community-based approaches.

1. Mato Oput: The Acholi people's traditional justice practice, Mato Oput, emphasizes reconciliation and compensation, reflecting restorative justice principles.

2. Legislative Support: Uganda's legal framework supports the use of restorative justice in addressing conflict and promoting peacebuilding.

3. Grassroots Initiatives: NGOs and community organizations in Uganda facilitate restorative justice practices, addressing the needs of victims and supporting offenders' reintegration.

Latin America

Brazil

Brazil has seen a growing adoption of restorative justice, particularly in its juvenile justice system.

1. Legislative Initiatives: Brazil's Child and Adolescent Statute promotes restorative justice practices for young offenders, emphasizing rehabilitation and social reintegration.

2. Restorative Circles: Restorative circles are used in schools and communities to address conflicts and promote healing.

3. Community Programs: Community-based restorative justice programs provide support and resources for victims and offenders, fostering a sense of community responsibility and collective healing.

Colombia

Colombia has integrated restorative justice into its efforts to address the legacy of conflict and promote peacebuilding.

1. Transitional Justice: Colombia's transitional justice framework includes restorative justice principles, focusing on truth, reparations, and reconciliation.
2. Community Reconciliation: Community-based restorative justice programs support reconciliation and healing in areas affected by violence and conflict.
3. Legislative Framework: Recent legal reforms have introduced restorative justice practices into Colombia's juvenile justice system, promoting rehabilitation and restorative outcomes.

Conclusion

The global adoption of restorative justice reflects a growing recognition of its effectiveness in addressing harm, promoting healing, and fostering social cohesion. Countries around the world have integrated restorative justice practices into their legal systems, supported by legislative frameworks, community programs, and cultural values. By emphasizing repairing harm, restoring relationships, and involving all stakeholders, restorative justice offers a transformative alternative to traditional punitive approaches. Subsequent chapters will delve deeper into the principles, practices, and impacts of restorative justice, providing further insights into its potential to create more just and compassionate societies.

Influential Figures and Movements

The revival and development of restorative justice in the modern era have been significantly shaped by various influential figures and movements. These individuals and organizations have played crucial roles in advocating for, researching, and implementing restorative justice practices worldwide. This chapter highlights key figures and movements that have been instrumental in shaping the restorative justice landscape.

Influential Figures in Restorative Justice

Howard Zehr

Howard Zehr is often referred to as the "grandfather" of restorative justice for his pioneering work and contributions to the field.

1. Key Contributions: Zehr's book, "Changing Lenses: A New Focus for Crime and Justice" (1990), provided a comprehensive framework for understanding restorative justice. His work emphasized viewing crime as a violation of people and relationships rather than just a breach of law.

2. Educational Impact: Zehr's teachings and writings have educated practitioners, policymakers, and the public about restorative justice, influencing the development of numerous programs and policies worldwide.

3. Center for Justice and Peacebuilding: Zehr has been a prominent figure at the Center for Justice and Peacebuilding

at Eastern Mennonite University, where he has continued to advocate for restorative justice through teaching and mentoring.

John Braithwaite

John Braithwaite, an Australian criminologist, has made significant theoretical contributions to restorative justice.

1. Reintegrative Shaming: Braithwaite introduced the concept of reintegrative shaming, which distinguishes between stigmatizing shaming (which alienates offenders) and reintegrative shaming (which condemns the crime but supports the offender's reintegration into society).

2. Restorative Justice and Responsive Regulation: His book, "Restorative Justice & Responsive Regulation" (2002), explores how restorative justice can be integrated into regulatory practices and criminal justice systems.

3. Global Influence: Braithwaite's research has influenced restorative justice practices and policies in various countries, promoting a more compassionate and effective approach to justice.

Mark Umbreit

Mark Umbreit is a leading practitioner and researcher in restorative justice, particularly in victim-offender mediation.

1. Victim-Offender Mediation: Umbreit has conducted extensive research on victim-offender mediation, demonstrating its effectiveness in promoting healing and reducing recidivism.

2. Center for Restorative Justice & Peacemaking: He founded the Center for Restorative Justice & Peacemaking at the University of Minnesota, which provides training, research, and resources for restorative justice practitioners.

3. Publications and Advocacy: Umbreit's numerous publications and advocacy efforts have significantly contributed to the global acceptance and implementation of restorative justice practices.

Kay Pranis

Kay Pranis is a notable figure in the development and promotion of restorative circles.

1. Circle Processes: Pranis has been instrumental in developing and promoting circle processes, a restorative practice that involves open dialogue and collective decision-making.

2. Training and Facilitation: She has provided extensive training for practitioners and facilitated circles in various contexts, including schools, communities, and the justice system.

3. Publications: Pranis has authored several influential books on circle processes, including "The Little Book of Circle Processes" (2005), which offers practical guidance for implementing circles.

Influential Movements and Organizations

The Restorative Justice Movement

The restorative justice movement has grown significantly since the 1970s, driven by grassroots advocacy, academic research, and policy development.

1. Grassroots Advocacy: Community organizations and advocates have played a crucial role in promoting restorative justice at the local level, developing programs that address specific community needs.

2. Academic Research: Academic institutions and researchers have conducted studies that demonstrate the effectiveness of restorative justice, providing a strong evidence base for its implementation.

3. Policy Development: Policymakers have increasingly recognized the benefits of restorative justice, leading to legislative support and the integration of restorative practices into formal justice systems.

Mennonite Central Committee (MCC)

The Mennonite Central Committee has been a pioneering organization in the promotion of restorative justice.

1. Early Programs: MCC initiated some of the first restorative justice programs, including the Victim-Offender Reconciliation Program (VORP) in Kitchener, Ontario, in 1974.

2. Advocacy and Education: MCC has continued to advocate for restorative justice and provide education and resources to support its implementation globally.

3. Global Impact: The organization's efforts have influenced the adoption of restorative justice practices in various countries, particularly in North America and Europe.

The European Forum for Restorative Justice (EFRJ)

The European Forum for Restorative Justice is a key organization promoting restorative justice across Europe.

1. Networking and Collaboration: EFRJ facilitates networking and collaboration among restorative justice practitioners, researchers, and policymakers across Europe.

2. Research and Advocacy: The organization supports research and advocacy efforts to promote restorative justice and influence policy development.

3. Training and Resources: EFRJ provides training, resources, and best practice guidelines to support the effective implementation of restorative justice practices.

The International Institute for Restorative Practices (IIRP)

The IIRP is a leading organization dedicated to the advancement of restorative practices worldwide.

1. Education and Training: IIRP offers a range of educational programs, including degrees and professional development courses, to train practitioners in restorative practices.

2. Research and Innovation: The institute conducts research to advance the field of restorative practices and develop innovative approaches to justice and conflict resolution.

3. Global Reach: IIRP has a global reach, with initiatives and partnerships in various countries to promote restorative practices in diverse contexts.

The United Nations (UN)

The United Nations has played a significant role in promoting restorative justice at the international level.

1. Endorsement and Guidelines: The UN has endorsed restorative justice principles and developed guidelines for their implementation, encouraging member

states to incorporate restorative practices into their justice systems.

2. Support for Member States: The UN provides support and resources to member states to develop and implement restorative justice programs, particularly in post-conflict and transitional justice contexts.

3. Global Advocacy: Through its various agencies and initiatives, the UN advocates for restorative justice as a means of promoting peace, reconciliation, and human rights.

Conclusion

The revival and development of restorative justice have been significantly shaped by influential figures and movements that have advocated for, researched, and implemented restorative practices worldwide. Individuals like Howard Zehr, John Braithwaite, Mark Umbreit, and Kay Pranis have made crucial contributions to the field, while organizations such as the Mennonite Central Committee, the European Forum for Restorative Justice, the International Institute for Restorative Practices, and the United Nations have played vital roles in promoting and supporting restorative justice globally. By highlighting the work of these key figures and movements, this chapter underscores the collective effort and impact that have propelled restorative justice to its current prominence, offering a transformative approach to justice that prioritizes healing, reconciliation, and community well-being. Subsequent chapters will explore the practical applications and outcomes of restorative justice in various contexts, providing further insights into its transformative potential.

CHAPTER 04

KEY PRINCIPLES OF RESTORATIVE JUSTICE

Victim-Centered Approach

Restorative justice is fundamentally victim-centered, prioritizing the needs, experiences, and well-being of victims. Traditional justice systems often marginalize victims, focusing primarily on punishing offenders. In contrast, restorative justice seeks to provide victims with a voice, support, and a sense of closure. This chapter examines how restorative practices center on victims, the benefits of this approach, and practical applications.

Understanding the Victim-Centered Approach

Principles of Victim-Centered Restorative Justice

1. Voice: Ensuring that victims have a platform to express their feelings, needs, and perspectives.

2. Support: Providing emotional, psychological, and practical support to help victims heal and recover.

3. Closure: Facilitating processes that enable victims to find closure and move forward.

Objectives of Victim-Centered Restorative Justice

1. Acknowledgment: Recognizing and validating the victim's experience and the harm they have suffered.

2. Empowerment: Empowering victims by involving them actively in the justice process.

3. Healing: Promoting emotional and psychological healing through supportive and restorative practices.

Benefits of a Victim-Centered Approach

Emotional and Psychological Healing

1. Validation of Experiences: Victims often feel validated when their experiences and emotions are acknowledged and respected.

2. Reduced Trauma: Engaging in restorative practices can reduce the trauma associated with crime by providing a safe space for victims to express their feelings.

3. Sense of Justice: Participating in restorative processes can help victims achieve a sense of justice and closure, contributing to their overall healing.

Increased Satisfaction with the Justice Process

1. Active Participation: Victims who participate in restorative justice processes often report higher satisfaction

with the justice system compared to those involved in traditional processes.

2. Fairness and Equity: The inclusive and respectful nature of restorative justice fosters a sense of fairness and equity, enhancing victim satisfaction.

3. Holistic Resolution: Restorative justice seeks to address the broader impact of crime on victims, providing a more comprehensive resolution.

Strengthened Relationships and Community Ties

1. Rebuilding Trust: Restorative practices can help rebuild trust between victims and offenders, as well as within the community.

2. Community Support: Involving the community in the restorative process fosters a supportive environment for victims, enhancing their sense of belonging and security.

3. Collective Healing: Restorative justice promotes collective healing by addressing the harm caused to both individuals and the community.

Practical Applications of a Victim-Centered Approach

Victim-Offender Mediation

Victim-offender mediation is a restorative practice that brings victims and offenders together to discuss the impact of the crime and agree on steps to repair the harm.

1. Facilitated Dialogue: A trained mediator facilitates the conversation, ensuring that the victim's voice is heard and respected.

2. Victim's Needs: The process prioritizes the victim's needs and seeks to address their concerns and desires for reparation.

3. Agreed Outcomes: Victims and offenders work together to reach mutually agreed-upon outcomes that promote healing and restitution.

Restorative Circles

Restorative circles involve victims, offenders, and community members in a structured dialogue aimed at healing and reconciliation.

1. Circle Format: Participants sit in a circle to promote equality and open communication. A talking piece is used to ensure everyone has an opportunity to speak.

2. Supportive Environment: The circle process creates a supportive environment where victims can express their feelings and receive empathy and support from others.

3. Collaborative Decision-Making: The group collaborates to develop a plan for addressing the harm and supporting the victim's healing process.

Family Group Conferencing

Family group conferencing involves the victim, the offender, their families, and community supporters in a meeting to address the harm and plan for the future.

1. Family Involvement: The victim's family is involved in the process, providing emotional support and contributing to the decision-making.

2. Holistic Support: The conference aims to provide holistic support for the victim, addressing their emotional, psychological, and practical needs.

3. Empowerment: Victims are empowered to take an active role in the process, ensuring that their needs and perspectives are prioritized.

Case Studies Illustrating a Victim-Centered Approach

Case Study 1: Healing through Mediation

In a case involving theft, the victim participated in a mediation session with the offender. The victim was able to express how the theft had impacted their life, and the offender acknowledged the harm caused. Through this process, the victim felt validated and was able to ask for restitution, which the offender agreed to provide. The mediation resulted in a sense of closure and healing for the victim.

Case Study 2: Restorative Circles in Schools

A high school implemented restorative circles to address bullying. Victims of bullying participated in circles with the offenders and other students. The process allowed victims to share their experiences and receive support from their peers. Offenders gained a deeper understanding of the impact of their actions and committed to making amends. The initiative led to a more supportive school environment and improved relationships among students.

Case Study 3: Family Group Conferencing for Domestic Violence

In the case of domestic violence, a family group conference was held involving the victim, the offender, their families, and community members. The victim was able to share their trauma and receive support from their family and community. The offender took responsibility for their actions and agreed to participate in a rehabilitation program. The conference facilitated a plan for ongoing support for the victim and accountability for the offender, promoting healing and reconciliation.

Challenges and Solutions in Implementing a Victim-Centered Approach

Overcoming Resistance to Participation

1. Building Trust: Establishing trust between facilitators and participants is crucial. Facilitators must create a safe and respectful environment.

2. Education and Awareness: Educating victims about the benefits of restorative justice can help overcome resistance and encourage participation.

3. Support Services: Providing access to support services, such as counseling and advocacy, can help victims feel more comfortable participating in restorative processes.

Ensuring Fairness and Equity

1. Addressing Power Imbalances: Facilitators must be trained to recognize and address power imbalances to ensure that victims' voices are heard and respected.

2. Neutral Facilitation: Facilitators must remain neutral and impartial, focusing on the needs and well-being of all participants.

3. Inclusive Practices: Implementing inclusive practices ensures that all affected parties have an equal opportunity to participate and contribute.

Conclusion

A victim-centered approach is a fundamental principle of restorative justice, prioritizing the needs, experiences, and well-being of victims. By providing victims with a voice, support, and a sense of closure, restorative justice promotes healing, empowerment, and satisfaction with the justice process. Practical applications such as victim-offender mediation, restorative circles, and family group conferencing illustrate how restorative practices can effectively address victims' needs and foster a supportive environment for healing and reconciliation. This chapter has explored the benefits and practical applications of a victim-centered approach, highlighting its transformative potential in creating a more just and compassionate justice system. Subsequent chapters will delve deeper into other key principles of restorative justice, providing further insights into its comprehensive and holistic approach.

Key Principles of Restorative Justice

Offender Accountability

Accountability is a cornerstone of restorative justice. This principle focuses on encouraging offenders to acknowledge their actions, understand their impact on victims and the community, and actively participate in making amends. Offender accountability is not about punishment but about fostering responsibility, empathy, and positive change. This chapter examines how restorative justice promotes offender accountability, its benefits, and practical applications.

Understanding Offender Accountability

Principles of Offender Accountability in Restorative Justice

1. Acknowledgment: Offenders must recognize and admit the harm they have caused.

2. Understanding Impact: Offenders need to understand the consequences of their actions on victims and the community.

3. Active Participation: Offenders are encouraged to take an active role in making amends and repairing the harm.

Objectives of Offender Accountability

1. Personal Responsibility: Encouraging offenders to take personal responsibility for their actions and their consequences.

2. Empathy Development: Fostering empathy by helping offenders understand the victim's perspective and the broader impact of their actions.

3. Positive Change: Promoting personal growth and positive change through active participation in restorative processes.

Benefits of Offender Accountability

Personal Growth and Rehabilitation

1. Understanding Consequences: By facing the impact of their actions, offenders gain a deeper understanding of the consequences, which is crucial for personal growth and rehabilitation.

2. Empathy and Remorse: Offender accountability fosters empathy and remorse, essential elements for genuine rehabilitation and behavior change.

3. Commitment to Change: Accountability processes encourage offenders to commit to positive change and avoid reoffending.

Restorative Justice for Victims

1. Validation: When offenders take responsibility, it validates the victims' experiences and acknowledges the harm they have suffered.

2. Sense of Justice: Seeing offenders held accountable can provide victims with a sense of justice and closure.

3. Restoration of Trust: Accountability helps restore trust between victims and offenders, paving the way for reconciliation and healing.

Community Benefits

1. Enhanced Public Safety: By addressing the root causes of criminal behavior and promoting rehabilitation, offender accountability contributes to enhanced public safety.

2. Community Healing: Community involvement in the accountability process fosters collective healing and social cohesion.

3. Reduced Recidivism: Offender accountability, coupled with support and rehabilitation, can lead to reduced recidivism rates, benefiting the broader community.

Practical Applications of Offender Accountability

Victim-Offender Mediation

Victim-offender mediation is a restorative practice that emphasizes offender accountability through direct dialogue between victims and offenders.

1. Facilitated Dialogue: A trained mediator facilitates the conversation, ensuring that offenders acknowledge their actions and understand their impact.

2. Offender Responsibility: Offenders are encouraged to take responsibility for their actions and express remorse to the victim.

3. Agreed Outcomes: Victims and offenders work together to reach mutually agreed-upon outcomes that promote healing and restitution.

Restorative Circles

Restorative circles involve victims, offenders, and community members in a structured dialogue aimed at accountability and healing.

1. Circle Format: Participants sit in a circle to promote equality and open communication. A talking piece is used to ensure everyone has an opportunity to speak.

2. Supportive Environment: The circle process creates a supportive environment where offenders can express remorse and commit to making amends.

3. Collaborative Decision-Making: The group collaborates to develop a plan for addressing the harm and supporting the offender's rehabilitation.

Family Group Conferencing

Family group conferencing involves the victim, the offender, their families, and community supporters in a meeting to address the harm and plan for the future.

1. Family Involvement: The offender's family is involved in the process, providing emotional support and contributing to the decision-making.

2. Holistic Support: The conference aims to provide holistic support for the offender, addressing their emotional, psychological, and practical needs.

3. Empowerment: Offenders are empowered to take an active role in the process, ensuring that their needs and perspectives are also considered.

Case Studies Illustrating Offender Accountability

Case Study 1: Theft and Restorative Mediation

In a case involving theft, the offender participated in a mediation session with the victim. The offender acknowledged the harm caused, expressed remorse, and agreed to provide restitution. Through this process, the offender gained a deeper understanding of the impact of their actions and committed to making positive changes to avoid reoffending.

Case Study 2: Restorative Circles in Schools

A high school implemented restorative circles to address incidents of bullying. Offenders participated in circles with their victims and other students. The process allowed offenders to understand the harm they caused and take responsibility for their actions. The initiative led to a reduction in bullying incidents and improved relationships among students.

Case Study 3: Domestic Violence and Family Group Conferencing

In a case of domestic violence, a family group conference was held involving the offender, the victim, their families, and community members. The offender took responsibility for their actions, expressed remorse, and agreed to participate in a rehabilitation program. The conference facilitated a plan for ongoing support for the victim and accountability for the offender, promoting healing and reconciliation.

Challenges and Solutions in Implementing Offender Accountability

Overcoming Resistance to Accountability

1. Building Trust: Establishing trust between facilitators and offenders is crucial. Facilitators must create a safe and respectful environment.

2. Education and Awareness: Educating offenders about the benefits of accountability can help overcome resistance and encourage participation.

3. Support Services: Providing access to support services, such as counseling and rehabilitation programs, can help offenders engage in the accountability process.

Ensuring Fairness and Equity

1. Addressing Power Imbalances: Facilitators must be trained to recognize and address power imbalances to ensure that the accountability process is fair and respectful.

2. Neutral Facilitation: Facilitators must remain neutral and impartial, focusing on the needs and well-being of all participants.

3. Inclusive Practices: Implementing inclusive practices ensures that all affected parties have an equal opportunity to participate and contribute.

Conclusion

Offender accountability is a fundamental principle of restorative justice, emphasizing the importance of acknowledging harm, understanding impact, and actively participating in making amends. By fostering personal responsibility, empathy, and positive change, restorative justice promotes healing and rehabilitation for offenders while providing validation and a sense of justice for victims. Practical applications such as victim-offender mediation, restorative circles, and family group conferencing illustrate how restorative practices can effectively promote offender accountability and foster a supportive environment for healing and reconciliation. This chapter has explored the benefits and practical applications of offender accountability, highlighting its transformative potential in creating a more just and compassionate justice system. Subsequent chapters will delve deeper into other key principles of restorative justice, providing further insights into its comprehensive and holistic approach.

Community Engagement

Restorative justice recognizes that crime affects not only individuals but also the broader social fabric. Engaging the community in the justice process is crucial for fostering collective healing, promoting social cohesion, and supporting both victims and offenders. This chapter explores the principles of community engagement in restorative justice, its benefits, and practical applications for fostering community involvement and support.

Understanding Community Engagement

Principles of Community Engagement in Restorative Justice

1. Collective Responsibility: Crime is seen as a violation of relationships within the community, and thus, the community has a role in addressing the harm and supporting healing.

2. Inclusivity: Engaging diverse community members ensures that all voices are heard and respected in the justice process.

3. Support and Accountability: The community provides both support for victims and offenders and holds offenders accountable in a constructive manner.

Objectives of Community Engagement

1. Social Cohesion: Strengthening social bonds and promoting a sense of belonging and mutual support within the community.

2. Collective Healing: Facilitating collective healing by addressing the broader impact of crime on the community.

3. Sustainable Reintegration: Supporting the reintegration of offenders into the community, reducing recidivism, and promoting long-term public safety.

Benefits of Community Engagement

For Victims

1. Support Network: Community involvement provides victims with a broader support network, helping them feel understood and cared for.

2. Restored Sense of Safety: Engaging the community in addressing the harm can help restore a sense of safety and security for victims.

3. Validation and Empowerment: Victims often feel validated and empowered when the community acknowledges their experiences and supports their healing.

For Offenders

1. Reintegration Support: Community engagement facilitates the reintegration of offenders, providing them with the resources and encouragement needed to make positive changes.

2. Accountability and Responsibility: Offenders are held accountable not only to their victims but also to the community, reinforcing the importance of taking responsibility for their actions.

3. Personal Growth: Positive social interactions and community support foster personal growth and rehabilitation for offenders.

For the Community

1. Strengthened Social Bonds: Community involvement in the justice process helps to strengthen social bonds, promoting trust, cooperation, and mutual support.

2. Increased Social Cohesion: Working together to address crime and support those affected enhances community cohesion and resilience.

3. Collective Healing: Community engagement promotes collective healing by addressing the harm caused to both individuals and the community as a whole.

Practical Applications of Community Engagement

Community Conferencing

Community conferencing involves bringing together victims, offenders, and community members to discuss the impact of the crime and develop a plan for repairing the harm.

1. Inclusive Participation: Community members are actively involved in the process, sharing their perspectives and contributing to the resolution.

2. Facilitated Dialogue: A trained facilitator guides the conversation, ensuring that all voices are heard and respected.

3. Collective Decision-Making: The group works together to develop a plan for repairing the harm and supporting the offender's reintegration.

Restorative Circles

Restorative circles involve victims, offenders, and community members in a structured dialogue aimed at healing and reconciliation.

1. Circle Format: Participants sit in a circle to promote equality and open communication. A talking piece is used to ensure everyone has an opportunity to speak.

2. Supportive Environment: The circle process creates a supportive environment where participants can express their feelings and receive empathy and support.

3. Collaborative Decision-Making: The group collaborates to develop a plan for addressing the harm and supporting the healing process.

Community Service

Community service is a form of reparation that involves offenders contributing to the community as a way of making amends for their actions.

1. Meaningful Contributions: Offenders engage in activities that benefit the community, such as cleaning up public spaces, helping with community projects, or providing assistance to those in need.

2. Building Positive Relationships: Through community service, offenders build positive relationships with community members, fostering trust and mutual respect.

3. Reintegration: Community service helps support the reintegration of offenders by providing them with opportunities to contribute positively to the community.

Case Studies Illustrating Community Engagement

Case Study 1: Community Healing after Vandalism

In a community affected by vandalism, restorative justice conferencing brings together the offenders, victims, and community members. The inclusive dialogue helped repair relationships within the community, with the offenders agreeing to repair the damage and participate in community service. This process strengthened community bonds and promoted a sense of collective responsibility.

Case Study 2: Support for Domestic Violence Survivors

A community-based restorative justice program provided support for survivors of domestic violence. Through restorative circles, survivors shared their experiences and received validation and support from the community. Offenders participated in community service and received ongoing support for rehabilitation. This approach fostered healing for survivors and promoted the reintegration of offenders.

Case Study 3: Reintegration after Theft

In a case involving theft, the offender participated in a community conferencing process with the victim and community members. The offender acknowledged the harm caused and committed to making restitution. Community members provided support and resources to help the offender reintegrate and make positive changes. This process promoted healing for the victim and supported the offender's rehabilitation.

Challenges and Solutions in Implementing Community Engagement

Overcoming Resistance to Community Involvement

1. Building Trust: Establishing trust among participants is crucial. Facilitators play a key role in creating a safe and respectful environment for dialogue.

2. Educating the Community: Educating community members about the benefits of restorative justice and their role in the process can help overcome resistance.

3. Providing Support: Ongoing support for victims, offenders, and community members is essential to ensure the success of restorative practices.

Ensuring Inclusive Participation

1. Addressing Power Imbalances: Facilitators must be trained to recognize and address power imbalances to ensure that all voices are heard and respected.

2. Maintaining Neutrality: Facilitators must remain neutral and impartial, focusing on the needs and well-being of all participants.

3. Inclusive Practices: Implementing inclusive practices ensures that all affected parties have an equal opportunity to participate and contribute.

Conclusion

Community engagement is a fundamental principle of restorative justice, emphasizing the active involvement of the community in the justice process. By fostering collective healing, promoting social cohesion, and supporting both victims and offenders, community engagement helps to create restorative communities where individuals are supported, harm is addressed, and relationships are restored. This chapter has explored the principles, benefits, and practical applications of community engagement in restorative justice, highlighting its potential to create a more just and compassionate society. Subsequent chapters will delve deeper into other key principles of restorative justice, providing further insights into its comprehensive and holistic approach.

Repairing Harm

The ultimate goal of restorative justice is to repair the harm caused by criminal behavior. This involves both tangible and intangible reparations, including apologies, restitution, and community service. By focusing on repairing harm, restorative justice aims to restore relationships, promote healing, and achieve a sense of justice for all parties involved. This chapter explores the principles of repairing harm, its benefits, and practical applications within restorative justice.

Understanding Repairing Harm

Principles of Repairing Harm in Restorative Justice

1. Acknowledgment: Recognizing and admitting the harm caused by the offender's actions.

2. Reparation: Taking steps to make amends and repair the damage caused by the crime.

3. Restoration: Focusing on restoring relationships and promoting healing for victims, offenders, and the community.

Objectives of Repairing Harm

1. Addressing Victims' Needs: Ensuring that victims' needs and concerns are prioritized in the justice process.

2. Promoting Accountability: Encouraging offenders to take responsibility for their actions and make meaningful reparations.

3. Fostering Healing and Reconciliation: Promoting healing and reconciliation among victims, offenders, and the community.

Benefits of Repairing Harm

For Victims

1. Validation and Closure: Victims often feel validated when their harm is acknowledged and addressed, leading to a sense of closure.

2. Restored Trust: Reparation efforts can help restore trust between victims and offenders, facilitating reconciliation.

3. Empowerment: Actively involving victims in the reparative process empowers them and recognizes their rights and needs.

For Offenders

1. Personal Growth and Rehabilitation: Taking responsibility for their actions and making amends fosters personal growth and rehabilitation for offenders.

2. Empathy and Remorse: Engaging in reparative actions helps offenders develop empathy and genuine remorse for their actions.

3. Positive Reintegration: Offenders who actively participate in repairing harm are more likely to reintegrate positively into their communities and avoid reoffending.

For the Community

1. Strengthened Social Bonds: Community involvement in the reparative process helps strengthen social bonds and promote collective healing.

2. Increased Social Cohesion: Working together to repair harm enhances community cohesion and resilience.

3. Collective Responsibility: The community plays a crucial role in supporting both victims and offenders, fostering a sense of collective responsibility and mutual support.

Practical Applications of Repairing Harm

Apologies

An apology is a fundamental aspect of repairing harm, providing a way for offenders to acknowledge their wrongdoings and express remorse.

1. Sincere Acknowledgment: Offenders must sincerely acknowledge the harm they have caused and take responsibility for their actions.

2. Expression of Remorse: A heartfelt apology includes expressing genuine remorse and regret for the impact of their actions on the victim and the community.

3. Commitment to Change: An effective apology involves a commitment to making positive changes to avoid repeating the harmful behavior.

Restitution

Restitution involves compensating the victim for the losses or damages caused by the offender's actions.

1. Financial Compensation: Offenders may be required to provide financial compensation to victims for their losses, such as medical expenses, property damage, or lost wages.

2. Service-Based Restitution: In some cases, offenders may provide restitution through services, such as repairing damaged property or performing specific tasks for the victim.

3. Symbolic Restitution: Symbolic restitution involves actions that symbolically address harm, such as community service or participating in programs that raise awareness about the consequences of crime.

Community Service

Community service is a form of reparation that involves offenders contributing to the community as a way of making amends for their actions.

1. Meaningful Contributions: Offenders engage in activities that benefit the community, such as cleaning up public spaces, helping with community projects, or providing assistance to those in need.

2. Building Positive Relationships: Through community service, offenders build positive relationships with community members, fostering trust and mutual respect.

3. Reintegration: Community service helps support the reintegration of offenders by providing them with opportunities to contribute positively to the community.

Case Studies Illustrating Repairing Harm

Case Study 1: Apology and Restitution after Theft

In a case involving theft, the offender participated in a mediation session with the victim. The offender acknowledged the harm caused and offered a sincere apology, expressing genuine remorse. Additionally, the offender agreed to provide financial restitution to compensate for the stolen items. The process led to a sense of closure and healing for the victim and fostered the offender's commitment to positive change.

Case Study 2: Community Service after Vandalism

A group of teenagers was involved in a vandalism incident that damaged public property. As part of their restorative justice process, the teenagers participated in community service, helping to repair the damage they had caused and engaging in other community improvement projects. This experience allowed them to understand the impact of their actions, build positive relationships with community members, and reintegrate into the community.

Case Study 3: Symbolic Restitution for Domestic Violence

In a case of domestic violence, the offender participated in a family group conference with the victim and their families. The offender acknowledged the harm caused, offered a heartfelt apology, and committed to attending a rehabilitation program. Additionally, the offender agreed to participate in community education programs to raise awareness about domestic violence. This approach facilitated healing for the victim and promoted positive change and accountability for the offender.

Challenges and Solutions in Implementing Repairing Harm

Overcoming Resistance to Reparative Actions

1. Building Trust: Establishing trust between facilitators and participants is crucial. Facilitators must create a safe and respectful environment.

2. Education and Awareness: Educating offenders about the benefits of reparative actions can help overcome resistance and encourage participation.

3. Support Services: Providing access to support services, such as counseling and rehabilitation programs, can help offenders engage in the reparative process.

Ensuring Fairness and Equity

1. Addressing Power Imbalances: Facilitators must be trained to recognize and address power imbalances to ensure that the reparative process is fair and respectful.

2. Neutral Facilitation: Facilitators must remain neutral and impartial, focusing on the needs and well-being of all participants.

3. Inclusive Practices: Implementing inclusive practices ensures that all affected parties have an equal opportunity to participate and contribute.

Conclusion

Repairing harm is a fundamental principle of restorative justice, emphasizing the importance of acknowledging harm, making amends, and promoting healing and reconciliation. By focusing on tangible and intangible reparations, restorative justice addresses the needs of victims, fosters personal growth and rehabilitation for offenders, and strengthens community bonds. Practical applications such as apologies, restitution, and community service illustrate how restorative practices can effectively repair harm and create a more just and compassionate justice system. This chapter has explored the benefits and practical applications of repairing harm, highlighting its transformative potential in fostering healing and restoring relationships. Subsequent chapters will delve deeper into other key principles of restorative justice, providing further insights into its comprehensive and holistic approach.

CHAPTER 05

THE IMPACT OF CRIME ON FAMILIES

Emotional and Psychological Effects

Crime can have profound emotional and psychological impacts on families. The ripple effects of criminal behavior extend beyond the immediate victim, affecting family dynamics, mental health, and overall well-being. This chapter discusses the various ways in which crime affects families emotionally and psychologically, highlighting the need for comprehensive support systems to address these challenges.

Understanding the Emotional and Psychological Impact

Emotional Turmoil

Crime often triggers a wide range of intense emotions within families, including fear, anger, sadness, and confusion.

1. Fear and Anxiety: Families may experience heightened fear and anxiety, worrying about their safety and the possibility of future crimes.

2. Anger and Resentment: Anger towards the offender and resentment about the disruption to their lives are common emotional responses.

3. Sadness and Grief: Families may grieve the loss of a sense of security, trust, and normalcy, leading to prolonged sadness and depression.

Psychological Trauma

The psychological impact of crime can be long-lasting, leading to various forms of trauma and mental health issues.

1. Post-Traumatic Stress Disorder (PTSD): Family members, particularly those who witnessed the crime or its aftermath, may develop PTSD, experiencing flashbacks, nightmares, and severe anxiety.

2. Depression: The emotional weight of crime can lead to clinical depression, characterized by persistent sadness, loss of interest in activities, and feelings of hopelessness.

3. Anxiety Disorders: Generalized anxiety disorder, panic attacks, and other anxiety-related conditions can arise from the stress and fear associated with crime.

Impact on Family Dynamics

Strained Relationships

Crime can strain family relationships, creating tension and conflict among family members.

1. Blame and Guilt: Family members may blame each other or themselves for the crime, leading to feelings of guilt and shame.
2. Communication Breakdowns: The stress and emotional turmoil can hinder open communication, causing misunderstandings and distancing within the family.
3. Trust Issues: Trust, both within the family and towards the outside world, can be severely compromised, making it difficult to maintain healthy relationships.

Role Changes and Responsibilities

Crime can disrupt traditional family roles and responsibilities, creating additional stress and challenges.

1. Caretaking Burden: In cases where a family member is injured or traumatized by the crime, other members may need to take on caretaking roles, adding to their emotional and physical burden.
2. Financial Strain: The financial impact of crime, such as medical expenses, legal fees, and lost income, can exacerbate stress and alter family dynamics.

3. Shift in Roles: Family members may have to adjust their roles and responsibilities to cope with the aftermath of the crime, leading to potential power struggles and resentment.

Mental Health Effects on Different Family Members

Impact on Children

Children are particularly vulnerable to the emotional and psychological effects of crime within their families.

1. Behavioral Changes: Children may exhibit behavioral changes such as aggression, withdrawal, or regression in developmental milestones.

2. Academic Performance: Stress and trauma can affect children's concentration and performance in school, leading to academic difficulties.

3. Emotional Distress: Children may experience intense emotional distress, including anxiety, depression, and feelings of insecurity.

Impact on Parents

Parents often bear the brunt of the emotional and psychological impact, as they try to support their children while dealing with their own feelings.

1. Parental Stress: The pressure to provide emotional and financial support can lead to heightened stress and burnout.

2. Mental Health Struggles: Parents may experience mental health issues such as anxiety, depression, and PTSD, impacting their ability to care for their children and themselves.

3. Strained Parental Relationships: The stress and emotional toll can strain relationships between parents, leading to conflict and potential separation or divorce.

Impact on Siblings

Siblings can also be deeply affected by crime within their families, often feeling neglected or burdened by additional responsibilities.

1. Jealousy and Resentment: Siblings may feel jealous or resentful of the attention given to the victimized family member, leading to feelings of neglect.

2. Protective Instincts: Older siblings may feel a heightened sense of responsibility to protect their younger siblings, adding to their emotional burden.

3. Emotional Spillover: The emotional and psychological effects on one sibling can spill over to others, creating a pervasive atmosphere of stress and anxiety.

Long-Term Psychological Effects

Chronic Stress

The long-term impact of crime can result in chronic stress, affecting the overall health and well-being of family members.

1. Physical Health Issues: Chronic stress can lead to physical health problems such as hypertension, heart disease, and weakened immune function.

2. Mental Health Disorders: Persistent stress increases the risk of developing mental health disorders such as anxiety, depression, and PTSD.

3. Reduced Quality of Life: The ongoing emotional and psychological burden can significantly reduce the quality of life for family members.

Intergenerational Trauma

The psychological impact of crime can extend across generations, affecting not only the immediate family but also future generations.

1. Inherited Trauma: Children and grandchildren may inherit the emotional scars of their ancestors, experiencing anxiety, depression, and other mental health issues.

2. Behavioral Patterns: Dysfunctional coping mechanisms and behavioral patterns can be passed down, perpetuating cycles of trauma and instability.

3. Family Legacy: The history of crime and its impact can become a part of the family narrative, influencing the identities and behaviors of future generations.

Support Systems for Addressing Emotional and Psychological Effects

Professional Counseling and Therapy

Access to professional counseling and therapy is crucial for addressing the emotional and psychological impact of crime on families.

1. Individual Therapy: Individual therapy provides a safe space for family members to process their emotions and develop coping strategies.

2. Family Therapy: Family therapy addresses relational dynamics and helps improve communication, support, and understanding within the family unit.

3. Trauma-Informed Care: Therapists trained in trauma-informed care can provide specialized support to address the specific needs of crime-affected families.

Community Support

Community support plays a vital role in helping families cope with the aftermath of crime.

1. Support Groups: Support groups offer a space for families to share their experiences, receive empathy, and learn from others who have faced similar challenges.

2. Community Resources: Access to community resources such as financial assistance, housing support, and legal aid can alleviate some of the burdens on affected families

3. Restorative Justice Programs: Participation in restorative justice programs can provide families with opportunities for dialogue, healing, and closure.

Self-Care and Resilience Building

Encouraging self-care and resilience-building practices can help families manage the emotional and psychological impact of crime.

1. Stress Management Techniques: Techniques such as mindfulness, meditation, and exercise can help family members manage stress and improve their overall well-being.

2. Healthy Coping Mechanisms: Developing healthy coping mechanisms, such as journaling, creative expression, and spending time in nature, can provide emotional relief and resilience.

3. Social Connections: Maintaining strong social connections with friends, extended family, and community members can provide essential emotional support and a sense of belonging.

Conclusion

The emotional and psychological effects of crime on families are profound and far-reaching. The impact extends beyond the immediate victim, affecting family dynamics, mental health, and overall well-being. By understanding these effects and implementing comprehensive support systems, we can better address the needs of crime-affected families and promote healing and resilience. This chapter has explored the various ways crime affects families emotionally and psychologically, highlighting the importance of professional counseling, community support, and self-care practices in mitigating these impacts. Subsequent chapters will delve deeper into other aspects of the impact of crime on families, providing further insights into how restorative justice can support healing and recovery.

The Impact of Crime on Families

Economic and Social Consequences

Beyond the emotional and psychological harm, crime can lead to significant economic hardship and social isolation for families and communities. These broader consequences can exacerbate the challenges faced by crime-affected families and hinder their ability to recover and rebuild. This chapter explores the economic and social consequences of crime, highlighting the ways in which they impact families and communities, and discusses potential strategies for mitigation and support.

Understanding Economic Consequences

Direct Financial Costs

Crime often results in immediate financial burdens for families.

1. Property Damage: Families may face the costs of repairing or replacing damaged or stolen property.

2. Medical Expenses: Injuries resulting from crime can lead to substantial medical bills, including emergency care, ongoing treatment, and rehabilitation.

3. Legal Fees: Legal proceedings, whether related to prosecuting the offender or seeking restitution, can incur significant legal costs.

Loss of Income

Crime can lead to a loss of income, further exacerbating financial difficulties for families.

1. Inability to Work: Victims who suffer physical or emotional trauma may be unable to work, resulting in lost wages.

2. Job Loss: In some cases, the impact of crime may lead to job loss, either because of the inability to perform job duties or due to the stigma associated with being a victim or offender.

3. Caregiving Responsibilities: Family members may need to take time off work to care for injured or traumatized relatives, leading to additional income loss.

Long-Term Financial Strain

The long-term financial impact of crime can be profound and enduring.

1. Debt Accumulation: The immediate costs of crime, combined with lost income, can lead to debt accumulation and financial instability.

2. Economic Disadvantage: Families affected by crime may experience long-term economic disadvantage, struggling to recover and build financial security.

3. Impact on Future Opportunities: The financial strain can limit future opportunities for education, employment, and overall economic mobility for family members.

Social Consequences

Social Isolation

Crime can lead to social isolation for both victims and offenders and their families.

1. Stigma and Shame: Victims and their families may experience stigma and shame, leading to withdrawal from social interactions and community activities.

2. Fear and Distrust: Fear of further victimization and distrust of others can result in social withdrawal and reduced community engagement.

3. Disconnection: Offenders and their families may also face social ostracism, further isolating them from community support and resources.

Impact on Community Relationships

The social fabric of communities can be significantly impacted by crime.

1. Erosion of Trust: Crime can erode trust among community members, making it difficult to maintain positive relationships and cooperate on community initiatives.

2. Community Cohesion: High levels of crime can weaken community cohesion, reducing the sense of belonging and mutual support among residents.

3. Neighborhood Safety: Perceptions of increased crime can lead to a decline in neighborhood safety and quality of life, prompting residents to relocate or disengage from community activities.

Broader Social Implications

Educational Impact

Crime can adversely affect educational outcomes for children and youth within affected families.

1. Attendance and Performance: Trauma and instability at home can lead to poor school attendance and academic performance.

2. Behavioral Issues: Children may exhibit behavioral issues in school, such as aggression, withdrawal, or difficulty concentrating, impacting their educational progress.

3. Limited Opportunities: The long-term financial and social impact of crime can limit educational opportunities, affecting future prospects and economic mobility.

Health and Well-Being

The broader social consequences of crime also extend to overall health and well-being.

1. Physical Health: Chronic stress and economic hardship can lead to various physical health issues, including hypertension, heart disease, and weakened immune function.

2. Mental Health: The ongoing emotional and psychological impact of crime can result in mental health disorders such as depression, anxiety, and PTSD.

3. Access to Services: Social isolation and economic strain can limit access to necessary health and support services, further exacerbating health issues.

Strategies for Mitigation and Support

Economic Support and Assistance

Providing economic support and assistance can help mitigate the financial impact of crime on families.

1. Financial Aid: Access to financial aid, such as emergency funds, grants, and low-interest loans, can help families cover immediate costs and stabilize their finances.

2. Employment Support: Programs that offer job training, placement services, and flexible work options can assist victims and their families in regaining financial stability.

3. Legal Assistance: Providing affordable or pro bono legal assistance can help families navigate legal proceedings and seek restitution without incurring significant costs.

Social Support and Community Engagement

Enhancing social support and community engagement can address the social consequences of crime.

1. Support Groups: Establishing support groups for victims, offenders, and their families can provide a space for sharing experiences, receiving empathy, and building supportive networks.

2. Community Programs: Community programs that promote social cohesion, such as neighborhood watch initiatives, community centers, and recreational activities, can help rebuild trust and engagement.

3. Restorative Justice Practices: Implementing restorative justice practices, such as community conferencing and restorative circles, can facilitate dialogue, healing, and reconciliation within the community.

Holistic Health and Well-Being

Promoting holistic health and well-being is crucial for addressing the broader social impact of crime.

1. Mental Health Services: Providing access to mental health services, including counseling and therapy, can help families cope with the emotional and psychological impact of crime.

2. Health and Wellness Programs: Programs that promote physical health, such as fitness classes, nutrition education, and stress management workshops, can improve overall well-being.

3. Access to Resources: Ensuring that families have access to necessary resources, such as healthcare, housing, and education, can support their recovery and resilience.

Case Studies Illustrating Economic and Social Consequences

Case Study 1: Economic Hardship after Burglary

In a case of residential burglary, the victim's family faced significant economic hardship. The burglary resulted in the loss of valuable items and property damage, leading to substantial financial costs. The family also experienced emotional distress and social isolation due to fear and distrust. Access to financial aid, legal assistance, and community support programs helped the family recover and rebuild their sense of security and well-being.

Case Study 2: Social Isolation after Violent Crime

A family affected by a violent crime experienced severe social isolation. The victim's trauma and fear of further victimization led to withdrawal from social activities and community engagement. The family also faced stigma and shame, further isolating them from their social network. Participation in support groups and restorative justice practices helped the family reconnect with their community, receive emotional support, and begin the healing process.

Case Study 3: Community Impact of Gang Violence

A neighborhood plagued by gang violence saw a decline in community cohesion and safety. Residents experienced fear, distrust, and social disconnection, leading to reduced participation in community activities. The economic impact included property damage and loss of business revenue. Community programs promoting social cohesion, neighborhood safety initiatives, and restorative justice practices helped address the broader social impact and rebuild trust and engagement within the community.

Conclusion

The economic and social consequences of crime are profound and far-reaching, affecting not only individual families but also the broader community. By understanding these impacts and implementing comprehensive support systems, we can better address the needs of crime-affected families and promote recovery and resilience. This chapter has explored the various economic and social consequences of crime, highlighting the importance of economic support, social engagement, and holistic health and well-being in mitigating these impacts. Subsequent chapters will delve deeper into other aspects of the impact of crime on families, providing further insights into how restorative justice can support healing and recovery.

Intergenerational Trauma

The effects of crime can ripple through generations, leaving lasting impacts on families long after the initial incident. This phenomenon, known as intergenerational trauma, involves the transmission of trauma from one generation to the next, affecting the emotional, psychological, and social well-being of descendants. This chapter examines the concept of intergenerational trauma, its mechanisms, and the importance of addressing it in restorative justice practices.

Understanding Intergenerational Trauma

Definition and Concept

Intergenerational trauma refers to the transmission of trauma from one generation to another. This can occur through various mechanisms, including genetic, psychological, and social pathways.

1. Genetic Transmission: Emerging research suggests that trauma can affect genetic expression, potentially passing on vulnerabilities to future generations through epigenetic changes.

2. Psychological Transmission: Traumatic experiences can influence parenting behaviors and family dynamics, leading to the replication of trauma-related behaviors and emotions in children.

3. Social Transmission: Trauma can shape family narratives, cultural practices, and community interactions, perpetuating cycles of trauma across generations.

Mechanisms of Intergenerational Trauma

1. Parental Influence: Parents who have experienced trauma may exhibit overprotectiveness, emotional unavailability, or maladaptive coping strategies, which can impact their children's development.

2. Family Dynamics: Dysfunctional family dynamics, such as poor communication, unresolved conflicts, and emotional suppression, can perpetuate trauma-related behaviors and emotions.

3. Cultural and Community Factors: Historical and collective traumas, such as those experienced by marginalized

communities, can be transmitted through cultural narratives, practices, and systemic inequalities.

Impact of Intergenerational Trauma

Emotional and Psychological Effects

Intergenerational trauma can lead to a range of emotional and psychological issues in descendants.

1. Anxiety and Depression: Descendants of trauma survivors may experience heightened levels of anxiety and depression, influenced by inherited vulnerabilities and family dynamics.

2. Post-Traumatic Stress Disorder (PTSD): Trauma-related symptoms, such as hypervigilance, flashbacks, and emotional numbness, can manifest in descendants, even if they have not experienced the original traumatic event.

3. Behavioral Issues: Intergenerational trauma can contribute to behavioral issues, including aggression, substance abuse, and self-harm, as individuals struggle to cope with unresolved emotions and stress.

Social and Relational Effects

The social and relational impact of intergenerational trauma can affect family dynamics and community interactions.

1. Trust and Attachment Issues: Descendants may struggle with trust and attachment, leading to difficulties in forming and maintaining healthy relationships.

2. Communication Challenges: Trauma can disrupt communication patterns within families, resulting in misunderstandings, conflict, and emotional distance.

3. Community Disconnection: The collective impact of trauma can lead to social isolation, reduced community engagement, and weakened social bonds.

Addressing Intergenerational Trauma in Restorative Justice

Importance of Addressing Intergenerational Trauma

1. Holistic Healing: Addressing intergenerational trauma is essential for holistic healing, ensuring that both the immediate and long-term impacts of crime are addressed.

2. Breaking the Cycle: Interventions aimed at addressing intergenerational trauma can help break the cycle of trauma, promoting resilience and positive outcomes for future generations.

3. Community Resilience: Supporting families in healing from intergenerational trauma can enhance community resilience, fostering stronger, more cohesive communities.

Strategies for Addressing Intergenerational Trauma

1. Trauma-Informed Care: Implementing trauma-informed care practices ensures that restorative justice processes are sensitive to the impacts of trauma and promote healing.

2. Family and Community Involvement: Engaging families and communities in restorative justice practices can help address the broader impact of trauma and support collective healing.

3. Intergenerational Interventions: Developing interventions that specifically target intergenerational trauma, such as family therapy, community support groups, and culturally relevant healing practices, can promote long-term healing and resilience.

Case Studies Illustrating Intergenerational Trauma

Case Study 1: Historical Trauma in Indigenous Communities

Indigenous communities have experienced significant historical trauma due to colonization, forced assimilation, and systemic discrimination. These traumas have been transmitted across generations, leading to widespread mental health issues, substance abuse, and social disconnection. Restorative justice practices that incorporate traditional healing methods, community involvement, and trauma-informed care have shown promise in addressing intergenerational trauma and promoting community resilience.

Case Study 2: Family Therapy for Descendants of Holocaust Survivors

Descendants of Holocaust survivors often experience intergenerational trauma manifested as anxiety, depression, and PTSD. Family therapy that focuses on processing the trauma, improving communication, and fostering emotional connection has been effective in promoting healing and breaking the cycle of trauma within these families.

Case Study 3: Community Support for Families Affected by Domestic Violence

Families affected by domestic violence can experience intergenerational trauma, impacting children's emotional and psychological well-being. Community-based restorative justice programs that provide support groups, counseling, and educational resources for both parents and children have helped address the trauma and promote healthier family dynamics and resilience.

Challenges and Solutions in Addressing Intergenerational Trauma

Overcoming Stigma and Resistance

1. Building Trust: Establishing trust between facilitators and participants is crucial. Facilitators must create a safe and respectful environment.

2. Education and Awareness: Educating families about the impact of intergenerational trauma and the benefits of addressing it can help overcome stigma and resistance.

3. Cultural Sensitivity: Ensuring that interventions are culturally sensitive and relevant can increase acceptance and effectiveness.

Ensuring Accessibility and Inclusivity

1. Providing Resources: Access to resources such as counseling, support groups, and educational materials is essential for addressing intergenerational trauma.

2. Inclusive Practices: Implementing inclusive practices ensures that all affected parties have an equal opportunity to participate and benefit from restorative justice processes.

3. Long-Term Support: Providing ongoing support and follow-up can help sustain the healing process and promote long-term resilience.

Conclusion

Intergenerational trauma is a profound and complex issue that can perpetuate cycles of harm and impact families for generations. Addressing intergenerational trauma within restorative justice practices is essential for holistic healing, breaking the cycle of trauma, and promoting resilience. By understanding the mechanisms of intergenerational trauma and implementing targeted strategies, restorative justice can support families and communities in their journey toward healing and recovery. This chapter has explored the concept of intergenerational trauma, its impact, and the importance of addressing it in restorative justice practices. Subsequent chapters will delve deeper into other aspects of the impact of crime on families, providing further insights into how restorative justice can support healing and recovery.

CHAPTER 06

THE ROLE OF CONFERENCING IN RESTORATIVE JUSTICE

What is Restorative Justice Conferencing?

Restorative justice conferencing is a structured meeting between victims, offenders, and community members aimed at addressing the harm caused by crime and finding mutually agreeable ways to repair that harm. This process emphasizes dialogue, accountability, and community involvement, fostering a collaborative approach to justice that seeks to heal rather than simply punish. This chapter provides an in-depth look at the restorative justice conferencing process, including its principles, benefits, stages, and practical applications.

Principles of Restorative Justice Conferencing

Core Principles

1. Inclusion: Restorative justice conferencing involves all affected parties, including victims, offenders, and community members, ensuring that everyone's voice is heard.

2. Accountability: Offenders are encouraged to take responsibility for their actions and understand the impact of their behavior on others.

3. Reparation: The focus is on repairing the harm caused by the crime through agreed-upon actions that address the needs of the victims and the community.

4. Dialogue: Open and respectful dialogue is central to the conferencing process, promoting understanding and empathy among participants.

5. Collaboration: The process is collaborative, with participants working together to develop a plan for reparation and healing.

Benefits of Restorative Justice Conferencing

For Victims

1. Voice and Empowerment: Victims have the opportunity to express their feelings, share their experiences, and participate actively in the justice process.

2. Validation: The acknowledgment of their pain and suffering by the offender and the community can provide validation and a sense of justice.

3. Healing and Closure: The process can help victims achieve emotional healing and a sense of closure, knowing that steps are being taken to address the harm.

For Offenders

1. Understanding Impact: Offenders gain a deeper understanding of the consequences of their actions on victims and the community.

2. Responsibility and Accountability: The process encourages offenders to take responsibility for their behavior and make amends.

3. Rehabilitation and Reintegration: By participating in reparation and making positive changes, offenders are better prepared for rehabilitation and reintegration into the community.

For the Community

1. Strengthened Relationships: The process helps repair and strengthen relationships within the community, fostering trust and cooperation.

2. Collective Healing: Community involvement promotes collective healing and resilience, addressing the broader impact of crime.

3. Enhanced Safety and Cohesion: By addressing the root causes of crime and supporting offender rehabilitation, the community becomes safer and more cohesive.

Stages of Restorative Justice Conferencing

Preparation

1. Identifying Participants: All affected parties, including victims, offenders, and community members, are identified and invited to participate.

2. Pre-Conference Meetings: Facilitators meet with participants individually to explain the process, address concerns, and prepare them for the conference.

3. Setting Goals: The goals of the conference are established, focusing on addressing the harm and developing a plan for reparation.

The Conference

1. Opening: The facilitator opens the conference, outlines the process, and sets the tone for respectful and constructive dialogue.

2. Victim's Perspective: The victim is given the opportunity to speak first, sharing their experience and the impact of the crime on their life.

3. Offender's Perspective: The offender responds, acknowledging their actions and expressing their understanding of the impact on the victim and the community.

4. Community Input: Community members share their perspectives on the crime's impact and offer support to both the victim and the offender.

5. Dialogue and Discussion: A facilitated discussion follows, allowing participants to ask questions, express emotions, and work towards mutual understanding.

6. Developing a Plan: Participants collaboratively develop a plan for reparation, specifying actions the offender will take to address the harm and support their rehabilitation.

Post-Conference

1. Follow-Up Meetings: Facilitators hold follow-up meetings with participants to monitor progress and provide ongoing support.

2. Implementation of the Plan: The agreed-upon plan for reparation is implemented, with the offender taking concrete steps to repair the harm.

3. Evaluation and Closure: The process is evaluated to assess its effectiveness, and participants are given the opportunity to reflect on their experiences and achieve closure.

Practical Applications of Restorative Justice Conferencing

Victim-Offender Conferencing

Victim-offender conferencing is a common form of restorative justice conferencing that focuses on direct dialogue between the victim and the offender.

1. Facilitated Dialogue: A trained facilitator guides the conversation, ensuring that both the victim's and the offender's voices are heard and respected.

2. Reparation Plan: The victim and the offender work together to develop a plan for reparation, which may include apologies, restitution, and community service.

3. Supportive Environment: The process creates a supportive environment where both parties can express their feelings and work towards healing and resolution.

Family Group Conferencing

Family group conferencing involves the extended family and support networks of both the victim and the offender.

1. Family Involvement: Family members and supporters are actively involved in the process, providing emotional support and contributing to the resolution.

2. Collaborative Decision-Making: The group works together to develop a plan for repairing the harm and supporting the offender's rehabilitation.

3. Strengthening Family Bonds: The process helps to strengthen family and community bonds, promoting a sense of collective responsibility and support.

Community Conferencing

Community conferencing involves a broader group of community members who are affected by the crime.

1. Inclusive Participation: Community members participate in the process, sharing their perspectives and contributing to the resolution.

2. Collective Healing: The process promotes collective healing by addressing the harm caused to the community and fostering a sense of solidarity.

3. Building Resilience: By involving the community in the justice process, restorative justice helps to build community resilience and cohesion.

Case Studies Illustrating Restorative Justice Conferencing

Case Study 1: Healing After Theft

In a case involving theft, a restorative justice conference was held with the victim, the offender, and community members. The victim shared how the theft had impacted their life, and the offender acknowledged the harm caused. Together, they developed a plan for restitution and community service, fostering healing and reconciliation.

Case Study 2: Reconciliation after Domestic Violence

A family affected by domestic violence engaged in restorative justice conferencing. The victim shared their trauma, and the offender took responsibility for their actions. Family members provided support, and a plan for rehabilitation and ongoing support was developed. The process helped the family to heal and rebuild their relationships.

Case Study 3: Community Healing After Vandalism

In a community affected by vandalism, restorative justice conferencing brings together the offenders, victims, and community members. The inclusive dialogue helped to repair relationships within the community, with the offenders agreeing to repair the damage and participate in community service. This process strengthened community bonds and promoted a sense of collective responsibility.

Challenges and Solutions in Restorative Justice Conferencing

Overcoming Resistance to Participation

1. Building Trust: Establishing trust among participants is crucial. Facilitators play a key role in creating a safe and respectful environment for dialogue.

2. Educating Stakeholders: Educating stakeholders about the benefits of restorative justice conferencing can help overcome skepticism and resistance.

3. Providing Support: Ongoing support for victims, offenders, and community members is essential to ensure the success of restorative practices.

Ensuring Fairness and Equity

1. Addressing Power Imbalances: Facilitators must be trained to recognize and address power imbalances to ensure that all voices are heard and respected.

2. Maintaining Neutrality: Facilitators must remain neutral and impartial, focusing on the needs and well-being of all participants.

3. Inclusive Practices: Restorative justice practices should be inclusive, ensuring that all affected parties have an opportunity to participate meaningfully.

Conclusion

Restorative justice conferencing is a powerful tool for addressing the harm caused by crime, promoting healing, and fostering a sense of community and responsibility. By involving victims, offenders, and community members in a structured dialogue, restorative justice conferencing emphasizes accountability, reparation, and collective healing. This chapter has provided an in-depth look at the principles, benefits, stages, and practical applications of restorative justice conferencing, highlighting its transformative potential in creating a more just and compassionate society. Subsequent chapters will explore other aspects of restorative justice, providing further insights into its comprehensive and holistic approach.

The Role of Conferencing in Restorative Justice

Types of Conferencing

Restorative justice conferencing encompasses various types of structured meetings designed to address the harm caused by crime through dialogue and collaboration. These conferencing models include victim-offender mediation, family group conferencing, and community conferencing. Each type serves a unique purpose and involves different participants, but all share the common goal of promoting healing, accountability, and reparation. This chapter provides a detailed overview of these three types of conferencing.

Victim-Offender Mediation

Definition and Purpose

Victim-offender mediation is a restorative justice process that facilitates direct dialogue between the victim and the offender. The primary goal is to allow victims to express their feelings, ask questions, and receive answers, while offenders have the opportunity to take responsibility and make amends.

Process of Victim-Offender Mediation

1. Preparation: Both parties meet separately with a trained mediator to discuss the process, address any concerns, and prepare emotionally for the meeting.

2. Mediation Session: The mediation session brings the victim and the offender together in a controlled environment. The mediator facilitates the conversation, ensuring it remains respectful and constructive.

3. Dialogue: The victim shares the impact of the crime on their life, while the offender responds by acknowledging the harm caused. Both parties can ask questions and express their emotions.

4. Reparation Agreement: The session concludes with a discussion about how the offender can make amends. This may include an apology, restitution, or community service. The agreement is documented and signed by both parties.

Benefits of Victim-Offender Mediation

1. Empowerment for Victims: Victims gain a voice in the justice process, allowing them to express their feelings and seek answers directly from the offender.

2. Accountability for Offenders: Offenders are encouraged to take responsibility for their actions and understand the impact of their behavior on the victim.

3. Healing and Closure: The process promotes emotional healing and closure for both victims and offenders, fostering a sense of justice and resolution.

Case Study: Healing through Direct Dialogue

In a case of burglary, the victim participated in a mediation session with the offender. The victim expressed their fear and distress caused by the crime, while the offender acknowledged the harm and apologized sincerely. The offender agreed to provide financial restitution and perform community service. This process helped the victim achieve a sense of closure and allowed the offender to take responsibility and make positive changes.

Family Group Conferencing

Definition and Purpose

Family group conferencing involves the victim, the offender, their extended families, and community support in a restorative meeting. The aim is to leverage family and community resources to address the harm, support the victim, and facilitate the offender's rehabilitation.

Process of Family Group Conferencing

1. Preparation: Facilitators meet with the victim, the offender, and their families separately to explain the process, address concerns, and prepare them for the conference.

2. Family Conference: The conference brings together all parties in a supportive environment. A trained facilitator guides the discussion, ensuring everyone has the opportunity to speak.

3. Dialogue and Support: The victim and the offender share their experiences and feelings. Family members and community supporters provide emotional support and contribute to the discussion.

4. Developing a Plan: Participants collaboratively develop a plan to address the harm, which may include restitution, community service, counseling, or other supportive measures. The plan is agreed upon and documented.

Benefits of Family Group Conferencing

1. Holistic Support: The involvement of family and community members provides a broader support network for both the victim and the offender.

2. Strengthening Family Bonds: The process can strengthen family relationships and promote collective responsibility for resolving the harm.

3. Comprehensive Reparation: The collaborative nature of the process ensures that the reparation plan addresses the needs of the victim, the offender, and the community.

Case Study: Rebuilding Family Trust

In the case of domestic violence, a family group conference was convened involving the victim, the offender, their children, and extended family members. The victim expressed their trauma and need for safety, while the offender took responsibility and committed to attending a rehabilitation program. Family members offered support and agreed to provide a safe environment for the victim. The process helped rebuild trust and foster a collective commitment to healing and change.

Community Conferencing

Definition and Purpose

Community conferencing engages the wider community in the restorative justice process. It involves victims, offenders, and community members in a structured dialogue aimed at addressing the harm and promoting collective healing.

Process of Community Conferencing

1. Preparation: Facilitators meet with the victim, the offender, and key community members separately to prepare them for the conference and address any concerns.

2. Community Conference: The conference brings together all participants in a neutral location. A trained facilitator guides the discussion, ensuring that all voices are heard and respected.

3. Open Dialogue: The victim and the offender share their experiences and feelings, while community members provide their perspectives on the impact of the crime. The discussion focuses on understanding the harm and identifying ways to repair it.

4. Developing a Community Plan: Participants collaboratively develop a plan to address the harm, which may include restitution, community service, or other restorative actions. The plan is agreed upon and documented.

Benefits of Community Conferencing

1. Collective Healing: The involvement of the community promotes collective healing and fosters a sense of solidarity and mutual support.

2. Enhanced Accountability: Offenders are held accountable not only to the victim but also to the community, reinforcing the importance of responsible behavior.

3. Building Resilience: Community conferencing helps build community resilience by addressing the root causes of crime and promoting social cohesion.

Case Study: Community Response to Vandalism

In a neighborhood affected by vandalism, a community conference was held involving the offenders, victims, and community members. The offenders acknowledged their actions and listened to the community members express their frustration and concerns. Together, they developed a plan that included restitution for the damaged property and participation in community beautification projects. The process helped heal the community and foster a sense of collective responsibility and pride.

Conclusion

Restorative justice conferencing encompasses various models that provide structured and supportive environments for addressing the harm caused by crime. Victim-offender mediation, family group conferencing, and community conferencing each offer unique benefits and approaches, but all share the common goal of promoting healing, accountability, and reparation. By involving victims, offenders, and community members in meaningful dialogue and collaborative decision-making, restorative justice conferencing fosters a more just and compassionate approach to justice. This chapter has provided an in-depth look at these types of conferencing, highlighting their processes, benefits, and practical applications. Subsequent chapters will explore other aspects of restorative justice, providing further insights into its comprehensive and holistic approach.

Benefits of Conferencing

Restorative justice conferencing offers numerous benefits for victims, offenders, and the broader community. By fostering dialogue, accountability, and mutual understanding, conferencing promotes healing and helps rebuild trust and relationships. This chapter outlines the various benefits of restorative justice conferencing, emphasizing enhanced understanding, empathy, and healing for all parties involved.

Enhanced Understanding

For Victims

1. Clarity and Answers: Victims often have unanswered questions about the crime and the motivations behind it. Conferencing provides an opportunity to ask these questions directly and gain clarity.

2. Understanding the Offender's Perspective: Through dialogue, victims can better understand the

offender's background, circumstances, and reasons for their actions, which can be crucial for emotional closure.

3. Insight into the Justice Process: Participating in the conferencing process helps victims understand the workings of restorative justice and their active role in seeking resolution.

For Offenders

1. Realization of Impact: Offenders gain a deeper understanding of the harm they have caused by hearing directly from victims and community members.

2. Personal Reflection: The process encourages offenders to reflect on their actions and the broader consequences, fostering a sense of responsibility and accountability.

3. Awareness of Community Norms: Engaging with community members helps offenders understand the values and norms of their community, which can guide their behavior moving forward.

For the Community

1. Understanding the Broader Impact: Community members gain insights into the ripple effects of crime, not just on the immediate victims but on the community as a whole.

2. Awareness of Collective Responsibility: The process highlights the role of the community in supporting

both victims and offenders, fostering a sense of collective responsibility.

3. Enhanced Communication: Community conferencing improves communication among residents, building a stronger, more informed community.

Empathy and Compassion

For Victims

1. Empathy from Offenders: Victims often feel validated when offenders express genuine remorse and empathy for their suffering.

2. Support from Community: The empathy and support shown by community members can provide emotional strength and reduce feelings of isolation.

3. Reduced Hostility: Understanding the offender's perspective can sometimes reduce feelings of hostility and anger, contributing to emotional healing.

For Offenders

1. Developing Empathy: Direct interaction with victims helps offenders develop empathy and compassion, understanding the real human impact of their actions.

2. Humanizing Victims: Offenders come to see victims as real people with emotions and lives affected by the crime, rather than abstract figures.

3. Motivation to Change: The empathy offenders feel can motivate them to make positive changes in their lives to avoid causing harm in the future.

For the Community

1. Building Compassionate Communities: Community involvement in the restorative process fosters a culture of empathy and compassion, strengthening social bonds.

2. Supporting Vulnerable Members: The process encourages community members to support those affected by crime, promoting collective well-being.

3. Reducing Prejudice: Increased empathy towards both victims and offenders helps reduce prejudice and stigma, fostering a more inclusive community.

Healing and Reconciliation

For Victims

1. Emotional Healing: The opportunity to express feelings, ask questions, and receive apologies can significantly contribute to victims' emotional healing.

2. Sense of Justice: Participating in a process that emphasizes accountability and reparation provides victims with a sense of justice and closure.

3. Restored Trust: Positive interactions with offenders and community members can help restore victims' trust in others and in the justice process.

For Offenders

1. Rehabilitation: Taking responsibility and making amends are critical steps in offenders' rehabilitation, helping them reintegrate into society.

2. Personal Growth: The process encourages personal growth and development, fostering positive changes in behavior and attitude.

3. Community Support: Engaging with community members who offer support and guidance can help offenders on their path to rehabilitation and reintegration.

For the Community

1. Community Healing: The process of addressing harm and working towards reparation fosters collective healing and strengthens community bonds.

2. Increased Safety: By addressing the root causes of crime and supporting offender rehabilitation, restorative justice conferencing contributes to a safer community.

3. Enhanced Cohesion: The process promotes social cohesion by encouraging collaboration, understanding, and mutual support among community members.

Practical Examples of Conferencing Benefits

Case Study 1: Restitution and Rehabilitation after Burglary

In a case involving burglary, the victim participated in a conferencing session with the offender and community members. The victim was able to express their fear and loss, while the offender acknowledged the harm and offered an apology. The community members provided support and helped develop a restitution plan that included financial compensation and community service. This process helped the victim achieve closure, the offender takes responsibility, and the community works together to support both parties.

Case Study 2: Healing and Empathy after Assault

A family group conference was held in a case of assault. The victim shared their trauma, and the offender, supported by their family, expressed deep remorse. The family members of both the victim and the offender participated, offering emotional support and contributing to a plan for rehabilitation and ongoing support. The process facilitated healing for the victim, accountability and personal growth for the offender, and strengthened family and community bonds.

Case Study 3: Community Cohesion after Vandalism

In a neighborhood affected by vandalism, a community conference was organized involving the offenders, victims, and community members. The offenders listened to the impact statements from the victims and community members, which helped them understand the broader consequences of their actions. The group collaboratively developed a plan for restitution and community beautification projects. This process promoted collective healing, reinforced community norms, and helped rebuild trust and cohesion within the community.

Conclusion

Restorative justice conferencing offers numerous benefits, including enhanced understanding, empathy, and healing for all parties involved. By fostering open dialogue, accountability, and collaboration, conferencing helps address the harm caused by crime and promotes a more just and compassionate society. This chapter has outlined the various benefits of restorative justice conferencing for victims, offenders, and the community, highlighting its transformative potential in promoting healing, reconciliation, and community cohesion. Subsequent chapters will explore other aspects of restorative justice, providing further insights into its comprehensive and holistic approach.

CHAPTER 07

CASE STUDIES OF RESTORATIVE JUSTICE CONFERENCING

Case Study 1: Reuniting a Family after Theft

Restorative justice conferencing can be a powerful tool for healing and reconciliation, especially within families torn apart by crime. This case study provides a detailed account of how restorative justice conferencing helped a family reconcile after a member committed theft. By focusing on dialogue, accountability, and mutual support, the process facilitated healing for the victim, accountability for the offender, and strengthened family bonds.

Background

The Incident

John, a 19-year-old college student, stole money from his younger sister, Emily, to fund his gambling habit. Emily discovered the theft when she noticed a significant amount of money missing from her savings, which she had been diligently putting aside for a school trip. The theft created a rift in the family, leading to distrust, anger, and emotional turmoil.

Family Dynamics

The family, consisting of John, Emily, their parents, and their grandmother, was deeply affected by the incident. Emily felt betrayed and unsafe, while the parents struggled with feelings of failure and guilt. John's actions caused tension and division, with the family uncertain about how to address the issue and move forward.

Initiating Restorative Justice Conferencing

Referral to Restorative Justice

The family was referred to a restorative justice program by a community mediator who believed that a structured conferencing process could help address the harm and facilitate reconciliation. The mediator explained the principles of restorative justice and obtained consent from all family members to participate in the conferencing process.

Preparation for the Conference

1. Pre-Conference Meetings: The facilitator held separate meetings with each family member to explain the process, discuss their concerns, and prepare them emotionally for the conference.

2. Setting Goals: The primary goals identified for the conference were to address the harm caused by the theft, provide a platform for open dialogue, and develop a plan for reparation and support for John's rehabilitation.

3. Building Trust: The facilitator worked to build trust among the family members, ensuring that they felt safe and respected throughout the process.

The Restorative Justice Conference

Opening the Conference

The conference was held at a neutral location to ensure a comfortable and safe environment for all participants. The facilitator opened the session by outlining the process and setting the ground rules for respectful and constructive dialogue.

Emily's Perspective

Emily was given the opportunity to speak first. She expressed her feelings of betrayal, anger, and fear, explaining how the theft had affected her sense of security and trust within the family. She also shared the emotional impact of losing her hard-earned savings, which had been earmarked for a special school trip.

John's Perspective

John listened attentively to Emily's account and then responded. He admitted to stealing the money, acknowledged the harm he had caused, and expressed deep remorse for his actions. John explained that his gambling addiction had driven him to theft and that he felt ashamed and guilty for betraying his sister and family.

Parents' and Grandmother's Perspectives

John and Emily's parents, along with their grandmother, shared their own feelings of hurt, disappointment, and concern. They expressed their sadness over the family discord and their worries about John's gambling problem. The parents also conveyed their love and commitment to supporting both John and Emily through the healing process.

Facilitated Dialogue

The facilitator guided the family through a structured dialogue, encouraging them to ask questions, express emotions, and seek understanding. This open communication allowed each family member to voice their feelings and needs, fostering empathy and mutual understanding.

Developing a Plan for Reparation

Collaborative Decision-Making

The family worked together to develop a plan for addressing the harm and supporting John's rehabilitation. The plan included:

1. Financial Restitution: John agreed to repay the stolen money to Emily in monthly installments, with a portion of his part-time job earnings dedicated to this purpose.

2. Counseling and Support: John committed to attending counseling sessions to address his gambling addiction and underlying issues. The family agreed to support him in this endeavor.

3. Family Support and Monitoring: The parents and grandmother pledged to provide ongoing emotional support and to monitor John's progress, ensuring he stayed on track with his commitments.

4. Rebuilding Trust: The family agreed to participate in regular family meetings to improve communication, rebuild trust, and address any ongoing concerns or issues.

Outcomes and Reflections

Emotional Healing

The restorative justice conference facilitated significant emotional healing for Emily. By expressing her feelings and receiving a sincere apology from John, she felt validated and began to regain a sense of security. The process also allowed her to see John's remorse and commitment to change, fostering forgiveness and empathy.

Accountability and Rehabilitation

John's participation in the conference and commitment to the reparation plan marked a turning point in his journey toward accountability and rehabilitation. The support from his family, coupled with counseling, helped him address his gambling addiction and work towards positive change.

Strengthened Family Bonds

The conferencing process helped rebuild trust and strengthen the bonds within the family. The open dialogue and collaborative decision-making promoted a sense of unity and mutual support, allowing the family to move forward together.

Lessons Learned

Importance of Preparation

Thorough preparation was crucial for the success of the conference. The pre-conference meetings helped each family member feel understood and prepared for the dialogue, ensuring a constructive and respectful process.

Role of the Facilitator

The facilitator played a key role in guiding the process, maintaining neutrality, and ensuring that all voices were heard.

Their expertise helped navigate the emotional complexities and fostered a safe environment for open communication.

Power of Dialogue and Empathy

The restorative justice conference highlighted the power of dialogue and empathy in addressing harm and promoting healing. By giving each family member a platform to express their feelings and needs, the process facilitated understanding, empathy, and reconciliation.

Conclusion

The case study of reuniting a family after theft demonstrates the transformative potential of restorative justice conferencing. By focusing on dialogue, accountability, and mutual support, the process facilitated healing for the victim, accountability for the offender, and strengthened family bonds. This chapter has provided a detailed account of how restorative justice conferencing can address harm and promote reconciliation within families, highlighting its benefits and practical applications. Subsequent chapters will explore other case studies and aspects of restorative justice, providing further insights into its comprehensive and holistic approach.

Case Study 2: Healing after Domestic Violence

Domestic violence cases are particularly challenging and complex, requiring sensitive and structured approaches to address the harm and facilitate healing. This case study explores the process and outcomes of restorative justice conferencing in a domestic violence case, highlighting the challenges faced and the successes achieved through this approach. The focus is on fostering a safe environment for dialogue, accountability, and mutual support to promote healing for the victim, rehabilitation for the offender, and resilience for the family.

Background

The Incident

Maria, a 32-year-old woman, experienced repeated physical and emotional abuse from her partner, David, over several years. The violence escalated to a point where Maria felt unsafe in her own home and decided to seek help. She reported the abuse to the authorities, leading to David's arrest and the initiation of legal proceedings.

Family Dynamics

Maria and David have two young children, aged 6 and 8, who were indirectly affected by the domestic violence. The children witnessed several incidents of abuse, which left them traumatized and anxious. Maria's extended family, including her parents and siblings, were deeply concerned for her safety and the well-being of the children.

Initiating Restorative Justice Conferencing

Referral to Restorative Justice

The case was referred to a restorative justice program by a social worker who believed that a structured conferencing process could help address the trauma, facilitate accountability, and support the family's healing. The social worker explained the principles of restorative justice to Maria, David, and their extended family, obtaining their consent to participate in the conferencing process.

Preparation for the Conference

1. Pre-Conference Meetings: The facilitator conducted separate meetings with Maria, David, their children, and extended family members to explain the process, address concerns, and prepare them emotionally for the conference.

2. Safety Planning: Ensuring Maria's safety was a top priority. A detailed safety plan was developed, including support from the social worker and legal protections, to ensure that Maria felt secure throughout the process.

3. Setting Goals: The primary goals identified for the conference were to address the harm caused by the abuse, provide a platform for open dialogue, develop a plan for David's rehabilitation, and support the family's healing and resilience.

The Restorative Justice Conference

Opening the Conference

The conference was held at a neutral and secure location, with additional security measures in place to ensure Maria's safety. The facilitator opened the session by outlining the process and setting ground rules for respectful and constructive dialogue.

Maria's Perspective

Maria was given the opportunity to speak first. She courageously shared her experiences of abuse, detailing the physical and emotional harm she had endured. Maria also expressed her concerns for the children's well-being and the impact of the violence on their emotional health.

David's Perspective

David listened to Maria's account with visible remorse. When it was his turn to speak, he admitted to the abuse, acknowledged the harm he had caused, and expressed deep regret for his actions. David explained that his behavior was influenced by unresolved anger issues and a lack of emotional control, which he now recognized needed addressing.

Children's Perspectives

The children, with the support of a child advocate, shared their feelings about the violence they had witnessed. They expressed fear, confusion, and sadness, highlighting how the abuse had affected their sense of security and trust within the family.

Extended Family's Perspectives

Maria's parents and siblings expressed their support for her and the children, sharing their own concerns and emotional distress caused by the situation. They also conveyed their willingness to support David's rehabilitation if it could lead to a safer and healthier family dynamic.

Facilitated Dialogue

The facilitator guided the family through a structured dialogue, encouraging them to ask questions, express emotions, and seek understanding. This open communication allowed each family member to voice their feelings and needs, fostering empathy and mutual understanding.

Developing a Plan for Reparation and Support

Collaborative Decision-Making

The family worked together to develop a comprehensive plan for addressing the harm and supporting David's rehabilitation. The plan included:

1. Counseling and Therapy: David committed to attending an intensive counseling program for anger management and emotional regulation. Maria and the children also agreed to participate in individual and family therapy to support their healing.

2. Safety Measures: A detailed safety plan was established, including regular check-ins with the social worker, legal protections, and clear boundaries to ensure Maria and the children's safety.

3. Parenting Support: Both Maria and David agreed to participate in parenting classes to improve their parenting skills and provide a stable and nurturing environment for the children.

4. Regular Family Meetings: The family agreed to hold regular meetings, facilitated by the social worker, to monitor progress, address ongoing concerns, and support open communication.

Outcomes and Reflections

Emotional Healing

The restorative justice conference facilitated significant emotional healing for Maria and the children. By expressing their feelings and receiving a sincere apology from David, they felt validated and began to regain a sense of safety and trust. The process also allowed them to see David's commitment to change, fostering hope for a healthier family dynamic.

Accountability and Rehabilitation

David's participation in the conference and commitment to the reparation plan marked a crucial step in his journey toward accountability and rehabilitation. The counseling program and family support helped him address his anger issues and develop healthier ways to manage his emotions and behavior.

Strengthened Family Bonds

The conferencing process helped rebuild trust and strengthen the bonds within the family. The open dialogue and collaborative decision-making promoted a sense of unity and mutual support, allowing the family to move forward together. The extended family's involvement provided additional support and reinforced the commitment to healing and positive change.

Challenges and Solutions

Overcoming Initial Resistance

1. Building Trust: Establishing trust among participants was crucial. The facilitator's expertise in creating a safe and respectful environment helped overcome initial resistance and fears.

2. Providing Comprehensive Support: Ensuring that Maria and the children had access to comprehensive support services, including counseling and legal protections, was essential for their participation and sense of safety.

Ensuring Fairness and Equity

1. Addressing Power Imbalances: The facilitator was trained to recognize and address power imbalances, ensuring that Maria and the children's voices were heard and respected throughout the process.

2. Maintaining Neutrality: The facilitator remained neutral and impartial, focusing on the needs and well-being of all participants.

Conclusion

The case study of healing after domestic violence demonstrates the transformative potential of restorative justice conferencing in addressing complex and sensitive issues. By focusing on dialogue, accountability, and mutual support, the process facilitated healing for the victim, accountability and rehabilitation for the offender, and strengthened family bonds. This chapter has provided a detailed account of how restorative justice conferencing can address the harm caused by domestic violence and promote reconciliation and resilience within families, highlighting the benefits and practical applications of this approach. Subsequent chapters will explore other case studies and aspects of restorative justice, providing further insights into its comprehensive and holistic approach.

Case Study 3: Restoring Community Trust

Community-wide incidents, such as acts of vandalism, violence, or systemic issues, can severely damage trust and relationships within a community. Restorative justice conferencing provides a powerful tool to address these issues by fostering dialogue, accountability, and collective healing. This case study explores how community conferencing was used to rebuild trust and relationships after a significant community-wide incident, highlighting the challenges faced and the successes achieved through this restorative approach.

Background

The Incident

In a small suburban neighborhood, a group of teenagers engaged in a series of vandalism acts that targeted public and private properties. The incidents included graffiti on community centers, damage to park facilities, and defacement of residential homes. The vandalism caused widespread anger, fear, and mistrust among residents, leading to a sense of division and insecurity within the community.

Community Dynamics

The neighborhood was a close-knit community where residents had traditionally enjoyed a strong sense of belonging and mutual support. The vandalism incidents disrupted this harmony, creating an atmosphere of suspicion and alienation.

Many residents felt personally violated, and there was a collective outcry for justice and reparation.

Initiating Community Conferencing

Referral to Restorative Justice

The community leaders, in collaboration with local law enforcement and a restorative justice organization, decided to initiate a community conferencing process. The goal was to address the harm caused by the vandalism, hold the offenders accountable, and restore trust and relationships within the community. Community members, including the victims and the offenders, were invited to participate in the conferencing process.

Preparation for the Conference

1. Pre-Conference Meetings: Facilitators held separate meetings with the offenders, the victims, and key community stakeholders to explain the process, address concerns, and prepare them emotionally for the conference.

2. Identifying Goals: The primary goals identified for the conference were to understand the impact of the vandalism, develop a plan for reparation, and foster a sense of community healing and reconciliation.

3. Building Trust: Facilitators worked to build trust among participants, ensuring they felt safe and respected throughout the process.

The Community Conference

Opening the Conference

The conference was held at a local community center to ensure accessibility and a neutral environment. The facilitator opened the session by outlining the process and setting ground rules for respectful and constructive dialogue.

Victims' Perspectives

Several community members who had been directly affected by the vandalism were given the opportunity to speak first. They shared their experiences of discovering the damage, the emotional distress it caused, and the sense of violation and insecurity they felt. Their accounts highlighted the broad impact of the vandalism on their personal lives and the community as a whole.

Offenders' Perspectives

The teenagers responsible for the vandalism, accompanied by their parents, listened to the victims' accounts with visible remorse. When given the opportunity to speak, the offenders admitted to their actions, acknowledged the harm caused, and expressed regret. They explained that their behavior was influenced by peer pressure and a lack of understanding of the consequences.

Community Members' Perspectives

Other community members, including local business owners and representatives of community organizations, shared their perspectives on the broader impact of the vandalism. They emphasized the loss of trust, the fear of further incidents, and the need for collective action to restore the sense of community.

Facilitated Dialogue

The facilitator guided the community through a structured dialogue, encouraging open communication and empathy. This allowed participants to ask questions, express emotions, and seek mutual understanding. The dialogue fostered a sense of solidarity and collective responsibility for addressing the harm.

Developing a Plan for Reparation and Community Building

Collaborative Decision-Making

The community worked together to develop a comprehensive plan for reparation and community building. The plan included:

1. Restitution and Restoration: The offenders agreed to participate in repairing the damaged properties, including repainting graffiti, fixing park facilities, and cleaning up affected areas. Community members volunteered to assist in these efforts.

2. Community Service: The offenders committed to participating in community service projects, such as organizing neighborhood clean-up events and helping with community center activities. This aimed to rebuild trust and demonstrate their commitment to making amends.

3. Educational Workshops: The community organized educational workshops on the consequences of vandalism and the importance of community values and respect. The offenders, along with other youth in the community, participated in these workshops to foster a better understanding of responsible behavior.

4. Ongoing Monitoring and Support: The community leaders, in collaboration with the restorative justice organization, established a monitoring and support system to ensure the ongoing engagement of the offenders in the reparation process and to provide continued support for their personal development.

Outcomes and Reflections

Rebuilding Trust

The community conferencing process played a crucial role in rebuilding trust within the neighborhood. By openly addressing the harm and working together on reparation projects, residents began to restore their sense of security and mutual respect. The visible efforts of the offenders to make amends helped to repair their relationships with the victims and other community members.

Promoting Accountability

The offenders' participation in the community conference and their commitment to the reparation plan demonstrated their accountability for their actions. The process encouraged them to reflect on their behavior, understand its impact, and take concrete steps to make positive changes. The support and guidance from the community also contributed to their rehabilitation and personal growth.

Strengthening Community Bonds

The collaborative efforts to address the vandalism and restore the community strengthened the bonds among residents. The shared experiences of working together on reparation projects and participating in educational workshops fostered a renewed sense of solidarity and collective responsibility. The process also highlighted the importance of community engagement in maintaining a safe and supportive environment.

Challenges and Solutions

Overcoming Initial Skepticism

1. Building Trust: Establishing trust among participants was essential. The facilitators' expertise in

creating a safe and respectful environment helped overcome initial skepticism and fears.

2. Educating the Community: Educating the community about the principles and benefits of restorative justice conferencing helped to build support and encourage participation.

Ensuring Inclusive Participation

1. Addressing Power Imbalances: The facilitators were trained to recognize and address power imbalances, ensuring that all voices were heard and respected throughout the process.

2. Maintaining Neutrality: The facilitators remained neutral and impartial, focusing on the needs and well-being of all participants.

Conclusion

The case study of restoring community trust through community conferencing demonstrates the transformative potential of restorative justice in addressing community-wide incidents. By focusing on dialogue, accountability, and collective action, the process facilitated healing for the victims, accountability and rehabilitation for the offenders, and strengthened community bonds. This chapter has provided a detailed account of how restorative justice conferencing can address the harm caused by community-wide incidents and promote reconciliation and resilience within communities, highlighting the benefits and practical applications of this approach. Subsequent chapters will explore other case studies and aspects of restorative justice, providing further insights into its comprehensive and holistic approach.

CHAPTER 08

STEPS TO IMPLEMENT RESTORATIVE JUSTICE CONFERENCING

Preparing for Conferencing

Assessment and Screening: Ensuring That Conferencing Is Appropriate for the Case

Before embarking on a restorative justice conferencing process, it is essential to conduct thorough assessment and screening to determine if the case is suitable for conferencing. This involves evaluating the readiness of the parties involved, the nature of the offense, and the potential benefits and risks of the conferencing process. Effective assessment and screening ensure that restorative justice conferencing is conducted in a safe, respectful, and productive manner, promoting healing and accountability.

Purpose of Assessment and Screening

Ensuring Suitability

1. Readiness of Participants: Assessing the emotional and psychological readiness of victims, offenders, and other participants to engage in the conferencing process.

2. Nature of the Offense: Evaluating whether the nature and context of the offense are appropriate for restorative justice conferencing.

3. Potential for Positive Outcomes: Determining whether the conferencing process is likely to achieve the desired outcomes of healing, accountability, and reparation.

Identifying Risks and Needs

1. Safety Concerns: Identifying any safety concerns or potential risks to participants and developing strategies to address them.

2. Support Needs: Identifying the support needs of participants, such as counseling, legal advice, or advocacy, to ensure they are adequately supported throughout the process.

3. Barriers to Participation: Identifying any barriers to participation, such as communication issues, power imbalances, or logistical challenges, and finding ways to mitigate them.

Steps in the Assessment and Screening Process

Initial Referral and Intake

1. Referral Source: The case may be referred to the restorative justice program by various sources, such as law enforcement, social services, schools, or community organizations.

2. Initial Contact: Program staff make initial contact with the referral source and gather basic information about the case, including the nature of the offense, the parties involved, and the context of the incident.

3. Intake Interview: An intake interview is conducted with the victim, the offender, and other relevant parties to gather detailed information and assess their initial willingness to participate in the conferencing process.

Evaluating Readiness

1. Victim Readiness: Assessing the victim's emotional and psychological readiness to participate in the conferencing process. This includes evaluating their desire for dialogue, their need for reparation, and their ability to engage constructively.

2. Offender Readiness: Assessing the offender's willingness to take responsibility for their actions, their understanding of the harm caused, and their commitment to making amends.

3. Family and Community Readiness: Assessing the readiness of family members and community participants to engage in the process and provide support.

Assessing the Nature of the Offense

1. Severity and Impact: Evaluating the severity of the offense and its impact on the victim, the offender, and the community. This includes considering physical, emotional, and psychological harm.

2. Context and Circumstances: Understanding the context and circumstances of the offense, including any contributing factors such as substance abuse, mental health issues, or social pressures.

3. Legal Considerations: Ensuring that the case is legally appropriate for restorative justice conferencing, including any requirements for confidentiality, consent, and compliance with legal standards.

Identifying Potential Benefits and Risks

1. Potential Benefits: Identifying the potential benefits of conferencing for the victim, the offender, and the community. This includes opportunities for healing, accountability, and relationship repair.

2. Potential Risks: Identifying potential risks, such as retraumatization, power imbalances, or safety concerns, and developing strategies to mitigate these risks.

3. Support Systems: Assessing the availability and adequacy of support systems for participants, such as counseling services, legal advice, and advocacy.

Developing a Plan for Conferencing

Safety Planning

1. Safety Assessment: Conducting a thorough safety assessment to identify any potential threats or risks to participants' physical and emotional safety.

2. Safety Strategies: Developing and implementing safety strategies, such as safety plans, secure locations, and support personnel, to ensure a safe environment for the conference.

3. Emergency Procedures: Establishing clear emergency procedures in case of any incidents during the conferencing process.

Addressing Support Needs

1. Counseling and Emotional Support: Ensuring that participants have access to counseling and emotional support before, during, and after the conference.

2. Legal and Advocacy Support: Providing access to legal advice and advocacy services to help participants understand their rights and responsibilities.

3. Logistical Support: Addressing any logistical needs, such as transportation, childcare, or accessibility accommodations, to facilitate participation.

Preparing Participants

1. Pre-Conference Meetings: Conducting individual meetings with each participant to explain the process, address concerns, and prepare them emotionally and psychologically for the conference.

2. Setting Expectations: Clearly outline the goals, ground rules, and expected outcomes of the conferencing process to ensure that all participants have a shared understanding.

3. Building Trust: Establishing trust and rapport with participants to create a safe and respectful environment for open dialogue and engagement.

Criteria for Proceeding with Conferencing

1. Willingness to Participate: Ensuring that all participants are willing to engage voluntarily in the conferencing process.

2. Readiness and Safety: Confirm that participants are emotionally and psychologically ready for the process and that safety measures are in place.

3. Support Systems in Place: Verifying that adequate support systems are available to address the needs of participants throughout the process.

4. Appropriateness of the Case: Determining that the nature of the offense and the context of the case are suitable for restorative justice conferencing.

Conclusion

Assessment and screening are critical steps in preparing for restorative justice conferencing. By thoroughly evaluating the readiness of participants, the nature of the offense, and the potential benefits and risks, facilitators can ensure that the conferencing process is appropriate, safe, and effective. This chapter has outlined the purpose, steps, and criteria for assessment and screening, highlighting their importance in promoting healing, accountability, and reparation. Subsequent chapters will explore other steps and aspects of implementing restorative justice conferencing, providing further insights into its comprehensive and holistic approach.

Steps to Implement Restorative Justice Conferencing

Participant Preparation: Preparing Victims, Offenders, and Community Members for the Process

Effective preparation of participants is crucial for the success of restorative justice conferencing. This involves ensuring that victims, offenders, and community members are emotionally, mentally, and practically ready to engage in the process. Proper preparation helps to foster a safe and respectful environment for dialogue, accountability, and healing. This chapter provides a comprehensive guide on how to prepare victims, offenders, and community members for restorative justice conferencing.

Objectives of Participant Preparation

1. Emotional Readiness: Ensuring that participants are emotionally prepared to engage in the process, express their feelings, and listen to others.

2. Understanding the Process: Providing participants with a clear understanding of the restorative justice process, including its goals, structure, and ground rules.

3. Building Trust and Safety: Establishing a foundation of trust and safety to ensure that participants feel secure and respected throughout the process.

Preparing Victims

Emotional and Psychological Support

1. Counseling Services: Offering access to counseling services to help victims process their emotions and prepare for the conference.

2. Emotional Safety: Ensuring that victims feel emotionally safe and supported, addressing any fears or concerns they may have about the process.

3. Empowerment: Empowering victims by reinforcing their role in the process and the importance of their voice and perspective.

Understanding the Process

1. Pre-Conference Meetings: Holding individual meetings with victims to explain the restorative justice process, its goals, and what to expect during the conference.

2. Explaining Roles: Clarifying the roles of all participants, including the victim's role, the offender's role, and the role of community members and facilitators.

3. Addressing Questions: Providing opportunities for victims to ask questions and address any uncertainties they may have about the process.

Practical Preparation

1. Logistics: Ensuring that victims have the necessary logistical support, such as transportation, childcare, and accessibility accommodations.

2. Safety Planning: Develop a safety plan to address any potential risks and ensure the victim's physical and emotional safety during the conference.

3. Support Person: Encouraging victims to bring a support person, such as a family member, friend, or advocate, to provide additional emotional support.

Preparing Offenders

Emotional and Psychological Support

1. Counseling Services: Providing access to counseling services to help offenders address any emotional or psychological issues and prepare for the conference.

2. Encouraging Accountability: Encouraging offenders to take responsibility for their actions and understand the impact of their behavior on the victim and the community.

3. Addressing Fears: Addressing any fears or concerns offenders may have about facing the victim and the community during the conference.

Understanding the Process

1. Pre-Conference Meetings: Hold individual meetings with offenders to explain the restorative justice process, its goals, and what to expect during the conference.

2. Explaining Roles: Clarifying the roles of all participants, including the offender's role in taking responsibility and making amends.

3. Addressing Questions: Providing opportunities for offenders to ask questions and address any uncertainties they may have about the process.

Practical Preparation

1. Logistics: Ensuring that offenders have the necessary logistical support, such as transportation and accessibility accommodations.

2. Support Person: Encouraging offenders to bring a support person, such as a family member, friend, or advocate, to provide additional emotional support.

3. Developing a Plan: Working with offenders to develop a preliminary plan for making amends, which can be further discussed and finalized during the conference.

Preparing Community Members

Emotional and Psychological Support

1. Understanding Impact: Helping community members understand the broader impact of the offense on the community and the importance of their participation in the process.

2. Encouraging Empathy: Encouraging community members to approach the process with empathy and an open mind, ready to listen and support both the victim and the offender.

3. Addressing Concerns: Addressing any concerns or fears community members may have about participating in the process.

Understanding the Process

1. Pre-Conference Meetings: Holding individual or group meetings with community members to explain the restorative justice process, its goals, and what to expect during the conference.

2. Explaining Roles: Clarifying the roles of all participants, including the community members' role in providing support and contributing to the reparation plan.

3. Addressing Questions: Providing opportunities for community members to ask questions and address any uncertainties they may have about the process.

Practical Preparation

1. Logistics: Ensuring that community members have the necessary logistical support, such as transportation and accessibility accommodations.

2. Support Network: Encouraging community members to connect with others who will be participating in the conference to build a supportive network.

3. Developing Contributions: Helping community members think about how they can contribute to the reparation plan and support both the victim and the offender.

Building Trust and Safety

Establishing Ground Rules

1. Respect and Confidentiality: Emphasizing the importance of respect and confidentiality throughout the process to create a safe environment for open dialogue.

2. Active Listening: Encouraging participants to practice active listening, allowing each person to speak without interruption and with full attention.

3. Non-Judgmental Approach: Promoting a non-judgmental approach, where participants are encouraged to understand and empathize with each other's perspectives.

Creating a Supportive Environment

1. Facilitator Role: The facilitator plays a crucial role in creating a supportive environment by remaining neutral, guiding the process, and addressing any issues that arise.

2. Safe Space: Ensuring that the physical space where the conference takes place is comfortable, neutral, and conducive to open dialogue.

3. Ongoing Support: Providing ongoing support to participants before, during, and after the conference to help them navigate the emotional challenges and maintain their commitment to the process.

Conclusion

Participant preparation is a critical step in ensuring the success of restorative justice conferencing. By thoroughly preparing victims, offenders, and community members, facilitators can create a safe, respectful, and productive environment for dialogue, accountability, and healing. This chapter has outlined the objectives, steps, and strategies for effective participant preparation, highlighting its importance in promoting positive outcomes for all parties involved. Subsequent chapters will explore other steps and aspects of implementing restorative justice conferencing, providing further insights into its comprehensive and holistic approach.

Conducting the Conference

Conducting a successful restorative justice conference requires careful planning and execution. The facilitator plays a crucial role in guiding the process, ensuring that all participants feel safe, respected, and heard. This chapter focuses on the importance of a skilled facilitator and outlines the key stages and activities during the conference.

Facilitator's Role

Importance of a Skilled Facilitator

1. Neutrality and Impartiality: The facilitator must remain neutral and impartial, ensuring that all participants are treated fairly and that their voices are equally valued.

2. Guiding the Process: A skilled facilitator guides the process, keeping the conversation on track and ensuring that the conference progresses through its key stages smoothly.

3. Creating a Safe Environment: The facilitator is responsible for creating and maintaining a safe environment where participants feel comfortable expressing their emotions and perspectives.

Key Responsibilities of the Facilitator

1. Pre-Conference Preparation: The facilitator conducts pre-conference meetings with each participant to explain the process, address concerns, and prepare them emotionally and practically for the conference.

2. Setting Ground Rules: At the beginning of the conference, the facilitator sets ground rules for respectful and constructive dialogue, emphasizing confidentiality, active listening, and non-judgmental communication.

3. Managing Dynamics: The facilitator manages the dynamics of the group, addressing any conflicts or tensions that arise and ensuring that the conversation remains respectful and productive.

4. Encouraging Participation: The facilitator encourages all participants to engage fully in the process, ensuring that everyone has an opportunity to speak and contribute to the discussion.

5. Summarizing and Clarifying: Throughout the conference, the facilitator summarizes key points and clarifies any misunderstandings to ensure that everyone has a clear understanding of the issues and agreements.

6. Supporting Emotional Needs: The facilitator provides emotional support to participants, acknowledging their feelings and helping them navigate difficult emotions that may arise during the conference.

Structure of the Conference

Key Stages and Activities

1. Opening the Conference

- Welcome and Introductions: The facilitator welcomes participants and introduces themselves, explaining their role and the purpose of the conference. Participants are then invited to introduce themselves.

- Setting Ground Rules: The facilitator sets ground rules for the conference, emphasizing the importance of respect, confidentiality, and active listening.

- Explaining the Process: The facilitator provides an overview of the restorative justice process, outlining the key stages and activities that will take place during the conference.

2. Sharing Perspectives

- Victim's Perspective: The victim is given the opportunity to speak first, sharing their experience of the offense and its impact on their life. This stage is crucial for validating the victim's feelings and setting the tone for the rest of the conference.

- Offender's Perspective: The offender responds, acknowledging their actions and expressing their understanding of the harm caused. This stage encourages accountability and empathy.

- Community Members' Perspectives: Community members share their perspectives on the impact of the offense on the community, providing additional context and support for both the victim and the offender.

3. Facilitated Dialogue

- Open Discussion: The facilitator guides an open discussion, encouraging participants to ask questions, express their emotions, and seek mutual understanding. This stage is essential for fostering empathy and building a shared understanding of the harm caused.

- Addressing Issues: The facilitator helps participants address any specific issues or concerns that arise during the discussion, ensuring that the conversation remains respectful and productive.

4. Developing a Reparation Plan

- Collaborative Decision-Making: Participants work together to develop a plan for reparation, focusing on actions the offender can take to make amends and support their rehabilitation. This may include apologies, restitution, community service, or other restorative actions.

- Documenting the Agreement: The facilitator ensures that the reparation plan is documented in detail, with clear responsibilities and timelines for implementation. All participants review and agree to the plan.

5. Closing the Conference

- Summary and Reflections: The facilitator summarizes the key points and agreements reached during the conference. Participants are invited to share their reflections on the process and their feelings about the outcomes.

- Next Steps: The facilitator outlines the next steps, including follow-up meetings or check-ins to monitor the implementation of the reparation plan and provide ongoing support.

- Closing Remarks: The facilitator thanks all participants for their contributions and commitment to the process, emphasizing the importance of continued communication and support.

Case Study: Conducting a Successful Conference

Scenario

In a case involving neighborhood vandalism, a restorative justice conference was organized to address the harm caused and rebuild community trust. The facilitator played a crucial role in guiding the process and ensuring a successful outcome.

Facilitator's Role

1. Pre-Conference Preparation: The facilitator conducted individual meetings with the victim, the offenders, and community members to explain the process, address concerns, and prepare them emotionally and practically for the conference.

2. Setting Ground Rules: At the beginning of the conference, the facilitator set ground rules for respectful and constructive dialogue, emphasizing confidentiality, active listening, and non-judgmental communication.

3. Managing Dynamics: Throughout the conference, the facilitator managed the dynamics of the group, addressing any conflicts or tensions that arose and ensuring that the conversation remained respectful and productive.

Structure of the Conference

1. Opening the Conference

- Welcome and Introductions: The facilitator welcomed participants and introduced themselves, explaining their role and the purpose of the conference. Participants then introduced themselves.

- Setting Ground Rules: The facilitator set ground rules for the conference, emphasizing the importance of respect, confidentiality, and active listening.

- Explaining the Process: The facilitator provided an overview of the restorative justice process, outlining the key stages and activities that would take place during the conference.

2. Sharing Perspectives

- Victim's Perspective: The victim shared their experience of discovering the vandalism, the emotional distress it caused, and the impact on their sense of security.

- Offender's Perspective: The offenders acknowledged their actions, expressed regret, and explained the factors that influenced their behavior.

- Community Members' Perspectives: Community members shared their perspectives on the broader impact of vandalism, emphasizing the loss of trust and the need for collective action to restore the sense of community.

3. Facilitated Dialogue

- Open Discussion: The facilitator guided an open discussion, encouraging participants to ask questions, express their emotions, and seek mutual understanding.

- Addressing Issues: The facilitator helped participants address specific issues, such as safety concerns and the need for increased community engagement.

4. Developing a Reparation Plan

- Collaborative Decision-Making: Participants worked together to develop a reparation plan, including actions the offenders could take to make amends, such as repairing the damaged property and participating in community service projects.

- Documenting the Agreement: The facilitator ensured that the reparation plan was documented in detail, with clear responsibilities and timelines for implementation.

5. Closing the Conference

- Summary and Reflections: The facilitator summarized the key points and agreements reached during the conference. Participants shared their reflections on the process and their feelings about the outcomes.

- Next Steps: The facilitator outlined the next steps, including follow-up meetings to monitor the implementation of the reparation plan and provide ongoing support.

- Closing Remarks: The facilitator thanked all participants for their contributions and commitment to the process, emphasizing the importance of continued communication and support.

Conclusion

Conducting a successful restorative justice conference requires the guidance of a skilled facilitator and a structured approach to ensure that all participants feel safe, respected, and heard. This chapter has highlighted the importance of the facilitator's role and outlined the key stages and activities during the conference, providing a comprehensive guide for effective conferencing. Subsequent chapters will explore other steps and aspects of implementing restorative justice conferencing, providing further insights into its comprehensive and holistic approach.

Follow-Up and Support

Post-conference support is crucial for the long-term success of restorative justice. Ensuring that participants receive adequate follow-up and ongoing support helps to reinforce the agreements made during the conference, promote healing, and prevent recidivism. This chapter explores the importance of follow-up and ongoing support for victims, offenders, and community members, detailing the strategies and activities involved in this critical phase.

Importance of Follow-Up and Support

1. Reinforcement of Agreements: Follow-up ensures that the commitments made during the conference are

honored and implemented, reinforcing the importance of accountability and responsibility.

2. Ongoing Healing: Continuous support helps victims, offenders, and community members process their emotions and experiences, promoting ongoing healing and reconciliation.

3. Prevention of Recidivism: Providing offenders with the necessary support and resources reduces the risk of reoffending, contributing to long-term community safety and stability.

4. Strengthening Relationships: Continued engagement and support help to rebuild and strengthen relationships among participants, fostering trust and cooperation within the community.

Strategies for Effective Follow-Up and Support

Monitoring Implementation

1. Regular Check-Ins: Facilitators or support workers conduct regular check-ins with participants to monitor the implementation of the reparation plan and provide ongoing support.

2. Progress Reports: Offenders provide progress reports on their compliance with the agreed-upon actions, such as restitution payments, community service, or participation in counseling programs.

3. Feedback Sessions: Participants are invited to provide feedback on the follow-up process, sharing their experiences, challenges, and any additional support needs.

Providing Emotional and Psychological Support

1. Counseling and Therapy: Access to counseling and therapy services is crucial for victims, offenders, and their families to continue processing their emotions and experiences.

2. Support Groups: Establishing support groups for victims, offenders, and community members provides a safe space for sharing experiences, receiving empathy, and building a support network.

3. Crisis Intervention: Providing access to crisis intervention services ensures that participants have immediate support in case of emotional or psychological crises.

Addressing Practical Needs

1. Resource Referrals: Facilitators refer participants to relevant resources and services, such as legal aid, financial assistance, housing support, or educational programs.

2. Employment and Education Support: Offenders receive assistance in finding employment or continuing their education, helping them to reintegrate into society and build a stable future.

3. Logistical Support: Ensuring that participants have access to transportation, childcare, or other logistical support to fulfill their commitments and attend follow-up meetings.

Key Activities in the Follow-Up Process

Individual Follow-Up Meetings

1. Victim Support: Individual follow-up meetings with victims focus on their emotional well-being, the implementation of the reparation plan, and any ongoing support needs.

2. Offender Support: Meetings with offenders address their progress in fulfilling the reparation plan, their participation in counseling or rehabilitation programs, and their overall adjustment and well-being.

3. Community Member Support: Follow-up meetings with community members provide an opportunity to discuss their perspectives on the process, the impact on the community, and any additional support they may need.

Group Follow-Up Sessions

1. Family Meetings: Facilitated family meetings help to address any ongoing issues, improve communication, and strengthen family relationships.

2. Community Gatherings: Organizing community gatherings fosters a sense of solidarity and mutual support,

allowing participants to share their progress and celebrate successes.

3. Restorative Circles: Holding restorative circles provides a structured space for participants to discuss their experiences, address any unresolved issues, and reinforce their commitment to the process.

Evaluating Progress and Outcomes

1. Outcome Assessment: Facilitators assess the outcomes of the restorative justice process, evaluating the effectiveness of the reparation plan and the overall impact on participants.

2. Feedback Collection: Gathering feedback from participants helps to identify areas of improvement and inform future restorative justice practices.

3. Reporting: Facilitators compile reports on the progress and outcomes of the follow-up process, sharing insights and recommendations with stakeholders and relevant authorities.

Case Study: Successful Follow-Up and Support

Scenario

In a case involving a neighborhood burglary, a restorative justice conference was held to address the harm caused and develop a reparation plan. The follow-up process played a crucial role in ensuring the success of the restorative justice outcomes.

Follow-Up Activities

1. Regular Check-Ins: The facilitator conducted monthly check-ins with the victim and the offender to monitor progress and provide ongoing support.

2. Counseling and Therapy: Both the victim and the offender receive counseling services to help them process their emotions and experiences.

3. Community Service and Restitution: The offender completed the agreed-upon community service hours and made regular restitution payments to the victim, demonstrating accountability and commitment to making amends.

4. Support Groups: The victim joined a support group for crime victims, while the offender participated in a group for individuals in rehabilitation, providing both additional emotional and social support.

Outcomes

1. Reinforced Accountability: The offender's consistent compliance with the reparation plan reinforced their accountability and commitment to positive change.

2. Ongoing Healing: The victim experienced ongoing emotional healing and felt supported throughout the process, leading to a sense of closure and security.

3. Community Trust: The follow-up activities helped to rebuild trust within the community, fostering a sense of solidarity and cooperation.

4. Long-Term Success: The comprehensive follow-up and support contributed to the long-term success of the restorative justice process, preventing recidivism and promoting community resilience.

Conclusion

Follow-up and support are essential components of a successful restorative justice process. By providing continuous monitoring, emotional and psychological support, and addressing practical needs, facilitators can ensure that participants remain committed to the process and achieve positive outcomes. This chapter has outlined the importance of follow-up and support, detailing the strategies and activities involved in this critical phase. Subsequent chapters will explore other steps and aspects of implementing restorative justice conferencing, providing further insights into its comprehensive and holistic approach.

CHAPTER 09

CHALLENGES AND SOLUTIONS IN RESTORATIVE JUSTICE

Common Challenges

Restorative justice conferencing can be a transformative process, but it also comes with various challenges that need to be addressed to ensure its effectiveness. This chapter identifies and addresses some of the most common challenges in restorative justice, including resistance from participants, power imbalances, and safety concerns. Understanding these challenges and developing strategies to overcome them is crucial for the success of restorative justice practices.

Resistance from Participants

Understanding Resistance

1. Fear and Anxiety: Victims and offenders may experience fear and anxiety about participating in the process, confronting each other, and discussing the crime and its impact.

2. Distrust in the Process: Participants may be skeptical about the restorative justice process, doubting its fairness, effectiveness, or relevance to their situation.

3. Reluctance to Change: Offenders might be resistant to acknowledging their wrongdoing and making amends, while victims may be hesitant to engage in a process they perceive as too lenient on offenders.

Strategies to Overcome Resistance

1. Building Trust and Rapport: Facilitators should focus on building trust and rapport with participants from the outset, demonstrating empathy, understanding, and commitment to a fair process.

2. Education and Information: Providing clear information about the restorative justice process, its goals, and benefits can help alleviate skepticism and build confidence in the process.

3. Support Services: Offering access to counseling and support services can help participants manage their fear and

anxiety, making them more comfortable with engaging in the process.

4. Voluntary Participation: Ensuring that participation is voluntary and that participants can opt-out at any time helps to reduce resistance and create a sense of empowerment.

Power Imbalances

Identifying Power Imbalances

1. Victim-Offender Dynamics: In many cases, there is an inherent power imbalance between victims and offenders, with victims feeling vulnerable and offenders potentially dominating the process.

2. Cultural and Social Factors: Cultural, social, and economic factors can also create power imbalances, affecting how participants interact and perceive each other.

3. Facilitator Authority: The facilitator's role and perceived authority can influence the dynamics of the process, potentially creating additional power imbalances.

Strategies to Address Power Imbalances

1. Facilitator Training: Facilitators should be trained to recognize and address power imbalances, ensuring that all participants are treated equitably and that their voices are equally valued.

2. Empowering Victims: Providing victims with additional support, such as legal advocacy, counseling, or

having a support person present, can help balance the power dynamics and ensure they feel safe and heard.

3. Creating Safe Spaces: Setting ground rules for respectful and non-judgmental communication helps create a safe space where participants can express themselves without fear of domination or retribution.

4. Cultural Competency: Facilitators should be culturally competent, understanding and respecting the cultural and social backgrounds of participants to address power imbalances effectively.

Safety Concerns

Identifying Safety Concerns

1. Physical Safety: Ensuring the physical safety of participants, especially victims, is paramount. This includes considering the location of the conference and potential threats from offenders or others.

2. Emotional Safety: Emotional safety is equally important, as the process can evoke strong emotions and potentially retraumatize participants.

3. Confidentiality Risks: Protecting the confidentiality of participants is crucial to ensure their safety and privacy throughout the process.

Strategies to Ensure Safety

1. Safety Planning: Developing a detailed safety plan for the conference, including secure locations, emergency procedures, and support personnel, helps to address physical safety concerns.

2. Emotional Support: Providing access to counseling and emotional support services before, during, and after the conference helps participants manage their emotions and feel supported.

3. Confidentiality Agreements: Ensuring that all participants sign confidentiality agreements helps to protect their privacy and create a safe environment for open dialogue.

4. Facilitator Vigilance: Facilitators must remain vigilant throughout the process, ready to intervene if any safety concerns arise and ensure that the process remains respectful and non-threatening.

Case Studies Illustrating Common Challenges

Case Study 1: Overcoming Resistance in a Theft Case

In a case involving theft, the victim initially resisted participating in the restorative justice process due to fear and skepticism. The facilitator spent additional time building trust with the victim, providing detailed information about the process, and addressing their concerns. Counseling services were offered, which helped the victim feel more secure and willing to engage. The process ultimately led to a successful resolution, with the victim feeling empowered and the offender taking responsibility for their actions.

Case Study 2: Addressing Power Imbalances in a Domestic Violence Case

A domestic violence case presented significant power imbalances between the victim and the offender. The facilitator ensured that the victim had a support person present and provided access to legal advocacy and counseling. Ground rules for respectful communication were established, and the facilitator remained vigilant in addressing any signs of domination or intimidation. These measures helped balance the power dynamics and allowed for a fair and equitable process.

Case Study 3: Ensuring Safety in a Vandalism Case

In a case of neighborhood vandalism, there were concerns about the physical and emotional safety of participants. The conference was held in a secure community center with emergency procedures in place. Confidentiality agreements were signed to protect participants' privacy, and counseling services were available to support emotional well-being. The facilitator maintained a safe environment, which enabled open and respectful dialogue, leading to a successful outcome.

Conclusion

Restorative justice conferencing can be highly effective in addressing harm and promoting healing, but it also comes with various challenges. By identifying and addressing common challenges such as resistance from participants, power imbalances, and safety concerns, facilitators can create a more effective and supportive restorative justice process. This chapter has outlined these challenges and provided strategies to overcome them, emphasizing the importance of preparation, support, and vigilance. Subsequent chapters will explore further aspects of implementing restorative justice conferencing, providing deeper insights into this comprehensive and holistic approach.

Solutions and Best Practices

To ensure successful restorative justice outcomes, it is essential to implement strategies and best practices that address common challenges and foster a supportive, effective process. This chapter outlines practical solutions and best practices for overcoming challenges such as resistance from participants, power imbalances, and safety concerns. By following these guidelines, facilitators can enhance the restorative justice experience and promote healing, accountability, and community cohesion.

Overcoming Resistance from Participants

Building Trust and Rapport

1. Personal Engagement: Facilitators should engage with participants on a personal level, demonstrating empathy, understanding, and commitment to a fair process. Establishing a connection can help alleviate fears and build trust.

2. Transparent Communication: Clear and open communication about the restorative justice process, its goals, and benefits helps participants understand what to expect and reduces skepticism.

3. Voluntary Participation: Emphasizing that participation is voluntary and that participants can opt-out at any time fosters a sense of empowerment and reduces resistance.

Providing Education and Information

1. Informational Sessions: Offering informational sessions or materials that explain the restorative justice process, its principles, and potential outcomes helps participants make informed decisions.

2. Success Stories: Sharing success stories and case studies from previous restorative justice processes can illustrate the benefits and effectiveness of the approach, building confidence in the process.

3. Addressing Misconceptions: Actively addressing and correcting any misconceptions or fears about restorative justice ensures that participants have a clear and accurate understanding of the process.

Offering Support Services

1. Counseling and Emotional Support: Providing access to counseling and emotional support services helps participants manage their fear and anxiety, making them more comfortable with engaging in the process.

2. Legal Advice and Advocacy: Offering legal advice and advocacy services ensures that participants understand their rights and feel supported throughout the process.

3. Peer Support: Encouraging peer support, where participants can connect with others who have been through the restorative justice process, can provide additional reassurance and encouragement.

Addressing Power Imbalances

Facilitator Training and Competence

1. Specialized Training: Facilitators should receive specialized training to recognize and address power imbalances, ensuring that all participants are treated equitably and that their voices are equally valued.

2. Cultural Competency: Facilitators should be culturally competent, understanding and respecting the

cultural and social backgrounds of participants to effectively address power imbalances.

3. Continuous Professional Development: Ongoing professional development and training opportunities help facilitators stay informed about best practices and new strategies for managing power dynamics.

Empowering Victims

1. Support Persons: Allowing victims to bring a support person, such as a family member, friend, or advocate, to provide additional emotional support and help balance power dynamics.

2. Legal and Advocacy Support: Providing access to legal and advocacy support ensures that victims understand their rights and have the resources they need to participate fully and confidently.

3. Emotional Preparation: Facilitators should work closely with victims to prepare them emotionally for the process, addressing any fears or concerns they may have.

Creating Safe and Equitable Spaces

1. Setting Ground Rules: Establishing clear ground rules for respectful and non-judgmental communication helps create a safe space where participants can express themselves without fear of domination or retribution.

2. Equal Speaking Time: Ensuring that all participants have equal speaking time during the conference helps prevent any one person from dominating the conversation.

3. Active Facilitation: Facilitators should actively manage the discussion, intervening when necessary to address power imbalances and ensure that all voices are heard and respected.

Ensuring Safety

Comprehensive Safety Planning

1. Physical Safety Measures: Develop a detailed safety plan that includes secure locations, emergency procedures, and support personnel to address any potential threats to participants' physical safety.

2. Emotional Safety Strategies: Providing access to counseling and emotional support services before, during, and after the conference to help participants manage their emotions and feel supported.

3. Confidentiality Protocols: Ensuring that all participants sign confidentiality agreements to protect their privacy and create a safe environment for open dialogue.

Ongoing Support and Monitoring

1. Regular Check-Ins: Facilitators or support workers should conduct regular check-ins with participants to monitor their well-being and provide ongoing support.

2. Crisis Intervention Services: Providing access to crisis intervention services ensures that participants have immediate support in case of emotional or psychological crises.

3. Follow-Up Meetings: follow-up meetings to review the implementation of the reparation plan, address any ongoing concerns, and provide additional support as needed.

Best Practices for Facilitators

Preparation and Planning

1. Thorough Preparation: Facilitators should thoroughly prepare for the conference by conducting pre-conference meetings with each participant, understanding their perspectives, and addressing any concerns.

2. Structured Process: Following a structured process with clearly defined stages helps ensure that the conference progresses smoothly and that all participants have an opportunity to contribute.

3. Flexibility and Adaptability: While following a structured process, facilitators should remain flexible and adaptable, responding to the needs and dynamics of the participants as they arise.

Active Facilitation

1. Neutrality and Impartiality: Maintaining neutrality and impartiality is crucial for building trust and ensuring that all participants feel heard and respected.

2. Empathy and Support: Demonstrating empathy and providing emotional support helps participants feel understood and valued, contributing to a more positive and productive process.

3. Conflict Resolution Skills: Facilitators should have strong conflict resolution skills to manage any conflicts or tensions that arise during the conference, ensuring that the discussion remains respectful and constructive.

Conclusion

Implementing restorative justice conferencing successfully requires addressing common challenges and following best practices. By building trust, providing education and support, addressing power imbalances, ensuring safety, and maintaining high standards for facilitation, restorative justice practitioners can create a more effective and supportive process. This chapter has outlined practical solutions and best practices for overcoming challenges and promoting positive outcomes in restorative justice conferencing, emphasizing the importance of preparation, support, and vigilance. Subsequent chapters will delve deeper into specific aspects and case studies of restorative justice, offering further insights into its comprehensive and holistic approach.

Policy and Legal Considerations

Restorative justice practices are influenced significantly by the legal and policy frameworks within which they operate. These frameworks can either support or hinder the implementation and effectiveness of restorative justice. This chapter examines the policy and legal considerations that affect restorative justice, discussing supportive policies, potential legal barriers, and strategies for navigating and improving these frameworks.

Supportive Policy and Legal Frameworks

Legislative Support

1. Restorative Justice Legislation: Some jurisdictions have specific legislation that mandates or encourages the use of restorative justice practices within the criminal justice system. This legal support can provide a clear mandate for restorative justice programs and help secure funding and resources.

2. Integration with Criminal Justice: Integrating restorative justice practices within the existing criminal justice framework, such as allowing judges to refer cases to restorative justice programs, can enhance the legitimacy and accessibility of these practices.

3. Youth Justice Policies: Policies that prioritize restorative justice for juvenile offenders can be particularly effective, recognizing the potential for rehabilitation and the importance of addressing harm in a constructive manner.

Policy Frameworks

1. National and Local Policies: National and local policies that explicitly support restorative justice can provide the necessary framework for implementation. These policies may include guidelines, funding provisions, and evaluation metrics to ensure effective practice.

2. Cross-Sector Collaboration: Policies that promote collaboration between various sectors, including law enforcement, social services, education, and community organizations, can enhance the implementation and impact of restorative justice practices.

3. Training and Development: Policies that mandate training and professional development for facilitators and other stakeholders ensure that restorative justice practices are implemented effectively and ethically.

Legal Barriers and Challenges

Lack of Legal Recognition

1. Absence of Legislation: In some jurisdictions, there may be a lack of specific legislation recognizing or supporting

restorative justice practices. This can limit the availability and legitimacy of restorative justice options within the formal justice system.

2. Inconsistent Application: Without clear legal frameworks, the application of restorative justice practices can be inconsistent, varying significantly between different regions or even within the same jurisdiction.

3. Judicial Reluctance: Judges and legal professionals may be reluctant to refer cases to restorative justice programs due to a lack of familiarity or confidence in these practices.

Confidentiality and Privacy Concerns

1. Legal Protections: Ensuring the confidentiality of restorative justice proceedings can be challenging, particularly when there is a need to balance transparency with privacy. Legal frameworks must provide clear guidelines on confidentiality protections for participants.

2. Privacy Laws: Privacy laws may restrict the sharing of information necessary for effective restorative justice processes. Navigating these legal constraints while ensuring the safety and privacy of participants is essential.

Accountability and Oversight

1. Regulatory Oversight: Effective regulatory oversight is necessary to ensure that restorative justice programs adhere to high standards of practice. This includes

establishing accreditation systems, regular evaluations, and accountability mechanisms.

2. Data Collection and Reporting: Legal frameworks should support the collection and reporting of data on restorative justice outcomes to ensure transparency, accountability, and continuous improvement.

Strategies for Navigating and Improving Legal and Policy Frameworks

Advocacy and Awareness

1. Raising Awareness: Advocating for restorative justice practices and raising awareness among policymakers, legal professionals, and the public can help build support for legislative and policy changes.

2. Building Coalitions: Forming coalitions of stakeholders, including community organizations, legal professionals, and victims' advocates, can strengthen advocacy efforts and increase the likelihood of policy change.

3. Educational Campaigns: Educational campaigns that highlight the benefits of restorative justice and provide evidence of its effectiveness can help shift public opinion and influence policymakers.

Policy Development and Reform

1. Drafting Legislation: Working with legislators to draft and promote restorative justice legislation can provide a

clear legal framework for implementation. This may include provisions for funding, training, and evaluation.

2. Policy Integration: Integrating restorative justice practices into existing policies and frameworks, such as juvenile justice or community safety strategies, can enhance their reach and impact.

3. Pilot Programs: Implementing pilot programs can demonstrate the effectiveness of restorative justice practices and provide a basis for broader policy adoption.

Training and Capacity Building

1. Professional Training: Providing comprehensive training for legal professionals, including judges, prosecutors, and defense attorneys, can increase their understanding and support for restorative justice practices.

2. Capacity Building for Facilitators: Investing in the training and professional development of restorative justice facilitators ensures that they have the skills and knowledge to implement practices effectively.

3. Cross-Sector Training: Promoting cross-sector training and collaboration among stakeholders, including law enforcement, social services, and community organizations, can enhance the coordination and effectiveness of restorative justice programs.

Case Studies of Policy and Legal Support

Case Study 1: Legislative Support in New Zealand

New Zealand has been a pioneer in integrating restorative justice into its legal system, particularly within its youth justice framework. The Children, Young Persons, and Their Families Act of 1989 established Family Group Conferences as a mandatory process for addressing youth offending. This legislative support has been instrumental in embedding restorative justice practices within the formal justice system, leading to positive outcomes for young offenders, victims, and communities.

Case Study 2: Policy Integration in Canada

Canada has also made significant strides in supporting restorative justice through policy integration. The Canadian Restorative Justice Consortium and various provincial initiatives have promoted the use of restorative justice practices across different sectors, including criminal justice, education, and community services. This integrated approach has helped to create a supportive environment for restorative justice, enhancing its accessibility and effectiveness.

Case Study 3: Advocacy and Reform in the United States

In the United States, advocacy efforts by organizations such as the National Association of Community and Restorative Justice have led to increased awareness and support for restorative justice practices. Several states, including Colorado and Vermont, have enacted legislation to support restorative justice programs, demonstrating the impact of sustained advocacy and policy reform efforts.

Conclusion

The implementation and effectiveness of restorative justice practices are significantly influenced by the legal and policy frameworks within which they operate. By understanding and navigating these frameworks, practitioners can overcome challenges and enhance the impact of restorative justice. This chapter has examined supportive policies, potential legal barriers, and strategies for improving legal and policy frameworks, emphasizing the importance of advocacy, training, and capacity building. Subsequent chapters will continue to explore the comprehensive and holistic approach of restorative justice, providing further insights and practical guidance for practitioners and stakeholders.

CHAPTER 10

THE FUTURE OF RESTORATIVE JUSTICE AND FAMILY REUNIFICATION

Emerging Trends

The field of restorative justice is continuously evolving, with new trends and innovations enhancing its effectiveness and reach. These emerging trends include technology-enhanced conferencing, global collaborations, and innovative approaches to family reunification. This chapter explores these trends, highlighting how they are shaping the future of restorative justice and offering new opportunities for healing and reconciliation.

Technology-Enhanced Conferencing

Virtual Conferencing Platforms

1. Accessibility and Convenience: Virtual conferencing platforms have made restorative justice more accessible by allowing participants to join from different locations. This is particularly beneficial for those who may have mobility issues, live in remote areas, or have scheduling constraints.

2. Overcoming Geographical Barriers: Technology allows for the inclusion of participants who are geographically dispersed, ensuring that all relevant parties can be involved in the restorative process.

3. Enhanced Communication Tools: Features such as video calls, chat functions, and document sharing enhance communication and facilitate a more interactive and engaging conferencing experience.

Data Management and Privacy

1. Secure Platforms: The use of secure, encrypted platforms ensures the confidentiality and privacy of participants, addressing concerns about data security.

2. Efficient Record-Keeping: Digital tools enable efficient record-keeping and documentation of restorative justice processes, which can be easily accessed and reviewed by authorized personnel.

3. Data Analytics: Advanced data analytics tools help in evaluating the effectiveness of restorative justice programs by analyzing trends, outcomes, and participant feedback.

Training and Capacity Building

1. Online Training Modules: Online training modules and webinars provide accessible and flexible training options for restorative justice facilitators, ensuring they have the necessary skills and knowledge.

2. Virtual Support Networks: Virtual support networks and communities of practice allow facilitators to share experiences, seek advice, and collaborate on best practices.

3. Simulation and Role-Playing: Virtual reality (VR) and augmented reality (AR) simulations offer immersive training experiences, helping facilitators develop their skills in a controlled and realistic environment.

Global Collaborations

International Restorative Justice Networks

1. Sharing Best Practices: International networks and collaborations facilitate the sharing of best practices, research findings, and innovative approaches across different cultural and legal contexts.

2. Cross-Cultural Learning: Engaging with restorative justice practitioners from diverse backgrounds promotes

cross-cultural learning and the adaptation of practices to suit local contexts.

3. Global Advocacy: International collaborations strengthen advocacy efforts by presenting a unified voice on the benefits and importance of restorative justice, influencing global policies and practices.

Cross-Border Initiatives

1. Joint Programs and Projects: Collaborative projects and programs between countries and regions enhance the reach and impact of restorative justice initiatives, addressing common challenges and sharing resources.

2. International Conferences and Workshops: Conferences and workshops provide platforms for practitioners, researchers, and policymakers to exchange ideas, showcase innovations, and build professional networks.

3. Global Research Partnerships: International research partnerships expand the evidence base for restorative justice, facilitating comparative studies and the development of globally relevant insights and recommendations.

Innovative Approaches to Family Reunification

Trauma-Informed Practices

1. Understanding Trauma: Integrating trauma-informed practices into restorative justice ensures that the processes are sensitive to the emotional and psychological

needs of participants, particularly in cases involving family reunification.

2. Holistic Support: Providing holistic support that addresses the emotional, psychological, and social dimensions of trauma promotes healing and long-term well-being for all family members.

3. Building Resilience: Trauma-informed restorative justice practices focus on building resilience, helping families develop coping strategies and strengthen their relationships.

Restorative Justice in Schools

1. Early Intervention: Implementing restorative justice programs in schools provides early intervention for conflicts and issues, promoting a culture of empathy, accountability, and mutual respect among students.

2. Family Engagement: School-based restorative justice programs often involve families, fostering stronger family-school partnerships and supporting family reunification efforts.

3. Educational Outcomes: By addressing conflicts and promoting a positive school climate, restorative justice in schools contributes to improved educational outcomes and student well-being.

Community-Based Approaches

1. Community Circles: Community circles bring together families, community members, and facilitators to address conflicts, share experiences, and develop collective solutions, fostering a sense of community and mutual support.

2. Supportive Networks: Building supportive networks within communities helps sustain the benefits of restorative justice, providing ongoing support and resources for families.

3. Cultural Relevance: Tailoring restorative justice practices to reflect the cultural values and traditions of the community enhances their relevance and effectiveness, promoting community buy-in and participation.

Case Studies of Emerging Trends

Case Study 1: Virtual Conferencing for Family Reunification

In a rural community with limited access to restorative justice services, virtual conferencing was implemented to facilitate family reunification after a domestic conflict. The use of a secure virtual platform allowed all family members, including those living in different states, to participate in the process. The virtual conferencing tools enabled real-time communication, document sharing, and facilitated dialogue. The process led to a successful resolution, demonstrating the potential of technology to enhance accessibility and engagement in restorative justice.

Case Study 2: International Collaboration on Juvenile Justice

A collaboration between restorative justice programs in Canada and South Africa focused on addressing juvenile justice issues. The partnership involved joint training programs, exchange visits, and the sharing of best practices. The initiative helped both countries improve their restorative justice approaches, integrating culturally relevant practices and addressing common challenges. The collaboration strengthened the global network of restorative justice practitioners and highlighted the benefits of cross-border partnerships.

Case Study 3: Trauma-Informed Practices in a School Setting

A school in the United States implemented a trauma-informed restorative justice program to address conflicts among students and support family reunification. The program included training for teachers and staff on trauma-informed practices, restorative circles for students and families, and ongoing counseling support. The initiative led to a significant reduction in disciplinary issues, improved student relationships, and enhanced family engagement, showcasing the effectiveness of trauma-informed restorative justice in educational settings.

Conclusion

Emerging trends and innovations in restorative justice, such as technology-enhanced conferencing, global collaborations, and innovative approaches to family reunification, are shaping the future of the field. These trends offer new opportunities for enhancing the accessibility, effectiveness, and reach of restorative justice practices. This chapter has explored these trends, highlighting their potential to transform restorative justice and promote healing, accountability, and community cohesion. Subsequent chapters will continue to delve into the future of restorative justice, providing further insights and practical guidance for practitioners and stakeholders.

The Future of Restorative Justice and Family Reunification

Expanding Applications

Restorative justice, traditionally used within the criminal justice system, has the potential to be applied in various other contexts, such as schools, workplaces, and communities. This chapter explores the expanding applications of restorative justice, highlighting its versatility and potential to address systemic issues across different settings. By examining these diverse applications, we can better understand how restorative justice can promote healing, accountability, and positive change in various environments.

Restorative Justice in Schools

Addressing Student Conflict

1. Conflict Resolution: Restorative justice practices can be used to address conflicts between students, such as bullying, fighting, and other behavioral issues. By facilitating dialogue and mutual understanding, these practices help resolve conflicts constructively.

2. Peer Mediation Programs: Schools can implement peer mediation programs where trained students facilitate restorative justice processes among their peers, promoting a culture of empathy and accountability.

3. Restorative Circles: Restorative circles provide a safe space for students to discuss conflicts, share their perspectives, and work together to develop solutions, fostering a supportive and inclusive school environment.

Enhancing School Climate

1. Building Relationships: Restorative justice practices focus on building positive relationships between students, teachers, and staff, creating a more cohesive and supportive school community.

2. Reducing Suspensions and Expulsions: By addressing behavioral issues through restorative practices rather than punitive measures, schools can reduce the rates of suspensions and expulsions, keeping students engaged in their education.

3. Promoting Inclusivity: Restorative justice promotes inclusivity by giving all students a voice and ensuring that their concerns are heard and addressed, creating a more equitable school environment.

Restorative Justice in Workplaces

Addressing Workplace Conflicts

1. Employee Disputes: Restorative justice can be used to address conflicts between employees, such as interpersonal disputes, harassment, and discrimination. By facilitating open dialogue and mutual understanding, these practices help resolve conflicts and improve workplace relationships.

2. Team Building: Restorative practices can be incorporated into team-building activities to strengthen relationships, improve communication, and foster a collaborative work environment.

3. Grievance Resolution: Organizations can implement restorative justice practices as part of their grievance resolution processes, providing a fair and

constructive way to address employee concerns and complaints.

Enhancing Workplace Culture

1. Promoting Respect and Accountability: Restorative justice fosters a workplace culture of respect and accountability, where employees are encouraged to take responsibility for their actions and work together to address issues.

2. Improving Morale and Engagement: By addressing conflicts and creating a positive work environment, restorative justice practices can improve employee morale and engagement, leading to higher job satisfaction and productivity.

3. Supporting Diversity and Inclusion: Restorative justice practices support diversity and inclusion by ensuring that all employees feel heard and valued, and by addressing systemic issues related to bias and discrimination.

Restorative Justice in Communities

Strengthening Community Bonds

1. Community Disputes: Restorative justice can be used to address disputes within communities, such as neighbor conflicts, property disputes, and issues related to community resources. By facilitating dialogue and mutual

understanding, these practices help resolve conflicts and strengthen community bonds.

2. Community Circles: Community circles provide a space for community members to discuss issues, share their perspectives, and work together to develop solutions, fostering a sense of community and mutual support.

3. Restorative Approaches to Crime: Communities can implement restorative justice practices to address crime and support both victims and offenders, promoting healing and reducing recidivism.

Promoting Community Engagement

1. Civic Participation: Restorative justice practices encourage civic participation by involving community members in decision-making processes and addressing community issues collaboratively.

2. Building Resilience: By fostering a culture of empathy, accountability, and mutual support, restorative justice practices help build resilient communities that can effectively address challenges and support their members.

3. Supporting Vulnerable Populations: Restorative justice can be used to support vulnerable populations within communities, such as the homeless, refugees, and individuals with mental health issues, by providing a compassionate and inclusive approach to addressing their needs.

Addressing Systemic Issues

Restorative Justice and Social Justice

1. Addressing Inequality: Restorative justice can be used to address systemic inequalities related to race, gender, socioeconomic status, and other factors by providing a platform for marginalized voices and promoting equity and inclusion.

2. Transformative Justice: Transformative justice extends beyond individual conflicts to address broader systemic issues, focusing on changing the underlying conditions that contribute to harm and injustice.

3. Policy Advocacy: Restorative justice practitioners can engage in policy advocacy to promote systemic changes that support restorative approaches and address the root causes of social issues.

Restorative Justice and Criminal Justice Reform

1. Alternatives to Incarceration: Restorative justice offers alternatives to incarceration by focusing on rehabilitation and reparation rather than punishment, reducing the reliance on punitive measures and addressing the root causes of criminal behavior.

2. Supporting Reentry: Restorative justice practices can support the reentry of formerly incarcerated individuals

by providing a framework for accountability, healing, and community reintegration.

3. Reducing Recidivism: By addressing the underlying issues that contribute to criminal behavior and promoting accountability and support, restorative justice practices can help reduce recidivism rates and promote long-term public safety.

Case Studies of Expanding Applications

Case Study 1: Restorative Justice in a High School

A high school in California implemented a restorative justice program to address student conflicts and improve school climate. The program included peer mediation, restorative circles, and professional development for teachers on restorative practices. As a result, the school saw a significant reduction in suspensions and expulsions, improved student relationships, and a more positive school environment.

Case Study 2: Restorative Justice in a Corporate Setting

A multinational corporation adopted restorative justice practices to address workplace conflicts and enhance its organizational culture. The company trained a team of internal facilitators to conduct restorative circles and mediation sessions. This approach led to a decrease in employee grievances, improved team cohesion, and higher employee engagement and satisfaction.

Case Study 3: Community-Based Restorative Justice Initiative

A community in the Midwest launched a restorative justice initiative to address neighborhood disputes and promote community engagement. The initiative included community circles, conflict resolution workshops, and partnerships with local organizations. The program successfully resolved several long-standing disputes, strengthened community bonds, and fostered a culture of mutual support and collaboration.

Conclusion

Restorative justice has the potential to be applied in various contexts, from schools to workplaces to communities, addressing conflicts, promoting healing, and fostering positive change. By exploring these expanding applications, we can better understand the versatility and transformative power of restorative justice. This chapter has highlighted how restorative justice can be used to address systemic issues and promote equity, inclusion, and community cohesion. Subsequent chapters will continue to delve into the future of restorative justice, providing further insights and practical guidance for practitioners and stakeholders.

Vision for the Future

Restorative justice has the potential to fundamentally transform the justice system and society as a whole. By shifting the focus from punishment to healing, accountability, and community engagement, restorative justice can create a more just, equitable, and compassionate world. This chapter provides a visionary look at the future of restorative justice, exploring its potential to reshape the justice system, influence societal values, and promote systemic change.

Transforming the Justice System

Integrating Restorative Justice into Mainstream Justice

1. Widespread Adoption: The future vision includes the widespread adoption of restorative justice practices within the mainstream justice system. This involves integrating restorative approaches at all stages of the justice process, from pre-trial diversion programs to post-sentencing rehabilitation.

2. Restorative Courts: Establishing dedicated restorative justice courts that handle specific types of cases, such as juvenile offenses, family disputes, and community conflicts, can provide a specialized and supportive environment for restorative practices.

3. Training and Education: Comprehensive training programs for judges, prosecutors, defense attorneys, and law enforcement officers will ensure that restorative justice

principles are understood and effectively implemented within the justice system.

Reducing Incarceration and Recidivism

1. Alternatives to Incarceration: Restorative justice offers viable alternatives to incarceration, focusing on rehabilitation and reparation rather than punishment. This can significantly reduce the prison population and the associated social and economic costs.

2. Rehabilitation and Reintegration: Restorative justice practices support the rehabilitation and reintegration of offenders by addressing the root causes of their behavior and promoting accountability and positive change.

3. Long-Term Public Safety: By addressing the underlying issues that contribute to criminal behavior and fostering a sense of community responsibility, restorative justice can enhance long-term public safety and reduce recidivism rates.

Influencing Societal Values

Promoting Empathy and Understanding

1. Cultural Shift: A future where restorative justice is widely practiced will see a cultural shift towards greater empathy, understanding, and compassion. By focusing on the human impact of crime and conflict, restorative justice

encourages people to see each other's perspectives and build stronger, more supportive communities.

2. Educational Integration: Integrating restorative justice principles into educational curricula from a young age can promote values of empathy, accountability, and conflict resolution, shaping the next generation's approach to justice and relationships.

3. Media and Public Awareness: Increasing media coverage and public awareness of restorative justice success stories can help change societal attitudes towards crime and punishment, fostering a more restorative mindset.

Building Stronger Communities

1. Community Engagement: Restorative justice practices emphasize community engagement and involvement, fostering a sense of collective responsibility and mutual support. This can lead to stronger, more resilient communities that are better equipped to address conflicts and challenges.

2. Social Capital: By building trust and social capital within communities, restorative justice can enhance social cohesion and create a more supportive and connected society.

3. Addressing Inequality: Restorative justice can play a role in addressing social inequalities by giving marginalized

voices a platform and promoting equitable solutions to conflicts and issues.

Promoting Systemic Change

Addressing Root Causes of Crime

1. Holistic Approaches: The future of restorative justice involves holistic approaches that address the root causes of crime, such as poverty, trauma, and lack of access to education and healthcare. By tackling these underlying issues, restorative justice can contribute to a more just and equitable society.

2. Policy Advocacy: Restorative justice practitioners and advocates can engage in policy advocacy to promote systemic changes that support restorative approaches and address the structural inequalities that contribute to crime and conflict.

3. Collaborative Solutions: Collaborative efforts between governments, non-profits, and communities can create comprehensive strategies to address the root causes of crime and promote restorative justice.

Enhancing Global Collaboration

1. International Networks: Building and strengthening international networks of restorative justice practitioners, researchers, and advocates can facilitate the exchange of ideas,

best practices, and innovations, enhancing the global impact of restorative justice.

2. Cross-Cultural Learning: Engaging in cross-cultural learning and collaboration can help adapt restorative justice practices to different cultural contexts, ensuring their relevance and effectiveness worldwide.

3. Global Advocacy: A unified global advocacy movement can promote restorative justice as a fundamental approach to justice and conflict resolution, influencing international policies and practices.

Case Studies of Visionary Practices

Case Study 1: Restorative City Initiatives

Several cities around the world, such as Hull in the UK and Oakland in the US, have embraced the concept of becoming restorative cities. These initiatives involve integrating restorative justice principles into various aspects of city governance, education, and community life. By promoting restorative practices across multiple sectors, these cities are creating a holistic approach to justice and community well-being, serving as models for other cities to follow.

Case Study 2: Restorative Schools Movement

The restorative schools movement is gaining momentum globally, with schools implementing restorative practices to address conflicts, build positive relationships, and create supportive learning environments. Schools that have adopted restorative justice report significant improvements in student behavior, reduced disciplinary actions, and enhanced school climate. This movement demonstrates the potential of restorative justice to transform educational settings and influence societal values.

Case Study 3: National Restorative Justice Policies

Countries like New Zealand and Norway have implemented national policies that support restorative justice practices, particularly within their juvenile justice systems. These policies provide a framework for integrating restorative approaches into the formal justice system, promoting rehabilitation and reducing recidivism. The success of these national initiatives highlights the potential for restorative justice to be scaled up and adopted at a broader policy level.

Conclusion

The future of restorative justice holds immense potential to transform the justice system and society. By integrating restorative practices into mainstream justice, influencing societal values, and promoting systemic change, restorative justice can create a more just, equitable, and compassionate world. This visionary look at the future of restorative justice highlights the importance of continued innovation, collaboration, and advocacy to realize this potential. Subsequent chapters will continue to explore the future of restorative justice, providing further insights and practical guidance for practitioners and stakeholders.

Vision for the Future

Restorative justice has the transformative potential to reshape the justice system and society as a whole. By focusing on healing, accountability, and community engagement rather than punishment, restorative justice can foster a more just, equitable, and compassionate world. This chapter presents a visionary look at the future of restorative justice, exploring its potential to revolutionize the justice system, influence societal values, and drive systemic change.

Transforming the Justice System

Integrating Restorative Justice into Mainstream Justice

1. Widespread Adoption: The vision for the future includes the widespread adoption of restorative justice practices within the mainstream justice system. This involves integrating restorative approaches at all stages, from pre-trial diversion programs to post-sentencing rehabilitation.

2. Restorative Justice Courts: Establishing dedicated restorative justice courts that handle specific types of cases, such as juvenile offenses, family disputes, and community

conflicts, can provide a specialized environment for restorative practices.

3. Training and Education: Comprehensive training programs for judges, prosecutors, defense attorneys, and law enforcement officers will ensure that restorative justice principles are understood and effectively implemented within the justice system.

Reducing Incarceration and Recidivism

1. Alternatives to Incarceration: Restorative justice offers alternatives to incarceration by focusing on rehabilitation and reparation rather than punishment. This approach can significantly reduce the prison population and the associated social and economic costs.

2. Rehabilitation and Reintegration: Restorative justice practices support the rehabilitation and reintegration of offenders by addressing the root causes of their behavior and promoting accountability and positive change.

3. Long-Term Public Safety: By addressing the underlying issues that contribute to criminal behavior and fostering a sense of community responsibility, restorative justice can enhance long-term public safety and reduce recidivism rates.

Influencing Societal Values

Promoting Empathy and Understanding

1. Cultural Shift: A future where restorative justice is widely practiced will see a cultural shift towards greater empathy, understanding, and compassion. By focusing on the human impact of crime and conflict, restorative justice encourages people to see each other's perspectives and build stronger, more supportive communities.

2. Educational Integration: Integrating restorative justice principles into educational curricula from a young age can promote values of empathy, accountability, and conflict resolution, shaping the next generation's approach to justice and relationships.

3. Media and Public Awareness: Increasing media coverage and public awareness of restorative justice success stories can help change societal attitudes towards crime and punishment, fostering a more restorative mindset.

Building Stronger Communities

1. Community Engagement: Restorative justice practices emphasize community engagement and involvement, fostering a sense of collective responsibility and mutual support. This can lead to stronger, more resilient communities that are better equipped to address conflicts and challenges.

2. Social Capital: By building trust and social capital within communities, restorative justice can enhance social cohesion and create a more supportive and connected society.

3. Addressing Inequality: Restorative justice can play a role in addressing social inequalities by giving marginalized voices a platform and promoting equitable solutions to conflicts and issues.

Promoting Systemic Change

Addressing Root Causes of Crime

1. Holistic Approaches: The future of restorative justice involves holistic approaches that address the root causes of crime, such as poverty, trauma, and lack of access to education and healthcare. By tackling these underlying issues, restorative justice can contribute to a more just and equitable society.

2. Policy Advocacy: Restorative justice practitioners and advocates can engage in policy advocacy to promote systemic changes that support restorative approaches and address the structural inequalities that contribute to crime and conflict.

3. Collaborative Solutions: Collaborative efforts between governments, non-profits, and communities can create comprehensive strategies to address the root causes of crime and promote restorative justice.

Enhancing Global Collaboration

1. International Networks: Building and strengthening international networks of restorative justice practitioners, researchers, and advocates can facilitate the exchange of ideas, best practices, and innovations, enhancing the global impact of restorative justice.

2. Cross-Cultural Learning: Engaging in cross-cultural learning and collaboration can help adapt restorative justice practices to different cultural contexts, ensuring their relevance and effectiveness worldwide.

3. Global Advocacy: A unified global advocacy movement can promote restorative justice as a fundamental approach to justice and conflict resolution, influencing international policies and practices.

Case Studies of Visionary Practices

Case Study 1: Restorative City Initiatives

Several cities around the world, such as Hull in the UK and Oakland in the US, have embraced the concept of becoming restorative cities. These initiatives involve integrating restorative justice principles into various aspects of city governance, education, and community life. By promoting restorative practices across multiple sectors, these cities are creating a holistic approach to justice and community well-being, serving as models for other cities to follow.

Case Study 2: Restorative Schools Movement

The restorative schools movement is gaining momentum globally, with schools implementing restorative practices to address conflicts, build positive relationships, and create supportive learning environments. Schools that have adopted restorative justice report significant improvements in student behavior, reduced disciplinary actions, and enhanced school climate. This movement demonstrates the potential of restorative justice to transform educational settings and influence societal values.

Case Study 3: National Restorative Justice Policies

Countries like New Zealand and Norway have implemented national policies that support restorative justice practices, particularly within their juvenile justice systems. These policies provide a framework for integrating restorative approaches into the formal justice system, promoting rehabilitation and reducing recidivism. The success of these national initiatives highlights the potential for restorative justice to be scaled up and adopted at a broader policy level.

Conclusion

The future of restorative justice holds immense potential to transform the justice system and society. By integrating restorative practices into mainstream justice, influencing societal values, and promoting systemic change, restorative justice can create a more just, equitable, and compassionate world. This visionary look at the future of restorative justice highlights the importance of continued innovation, collaboration, and advocacy to realize this potential. As restorative justice continues to evolve and expand, its principles and practices can pave the way for a more humane and effective approach to addressing crime and conflict.

CONCLUSION

RECAP OF KEY POINTS

Throughout this book, we have explored the profound impact of restorative justice on families, communities, and the broader justice system. By emphasizing healing, accountability, and community engagement, restorative justice offers a transformative approach to addressing crime and conflict. This chapter summarizes the key points discussed and their implications for families and communities.

Understanding Restorative Justice

Philosophical Foundations

Restorative justice is grounded in the principles of healing over punishment, inclusive dialogue, accountability, and community involvement. These core values distinguish it from traditional punitive approaches, focusing instead on repairing harm and restoring relationships.

Theological, Psychological, and Philosophical Perspectives

We examined restorative justice through various lenses, highlighting its alignment with theological principles of forgiveness and reconciliation, psychological benefits of trauma healing and emotional closure, and philosophical emphasis on justice as a relational concept.

The Importance of Family Reunification

Emotional and Psychological Effects

Crime deeply affects families, causing emotional and psychological distress. Restorative justice seeks to address these impacts by facilitating dialogue and understanding, ultimately promoting healing and reconciliation within families.

Economic and Social Consequences

Beyond emotional harm, crime can lead to economic hardship and social isolation. Restorative justice helps mitigate these consequences by fostering supportive environments and addressing practical needs.

Intergenerational Trauma

The ripple effects of crime can span generations. Addressing intergenerational trauma through restorative practices can break cycles of harm and foster resilience in families and communities.

The Role of Conferencing in Restorative Justice

Victim-Offender Mediation

Direct dialogue between victims and offenders allows for personal accountability and reparation. This process can be deeply healing for victims and transformative for offenders.

Family Group Conferencing

Involving extended family members and community support, family group conferencing addresses harm in a holistic manner, leveraging familial and community resources to support healing and rehabilitation.

Community Conferencing

Engaging the wider community in the restorative process promotes collective healing and reinforces community bonds. This approach recognizes that crime affects the broader social fabric and involves the community in finding solutions.

Benefits of Conferencing

Enhanced Understanding and Empathy

Restorative justice conferencing fosters mutual understanding and empathy among participants, helping them see the human impact of crime and conflict.

Healing and Reconciliation

The process promotes emotional healing and reconciliation, providing victims with a sense of closure and offenders with a path to rehabilitation.

Community Engagement and Support

Restorative justice emphasizes community involvement, strengthening social bonds, and fostering a sense of collective responsibility and support.

Implementing Restorative Justice

Preparation and Conducting of Conferences

Effective preparation of participants is crucial for the success of restorative justice conferencing. This involves ensuring emotional and practical readiness, setting ground rules, and facilitating structured dialogue.

Follow-Up and Support

Post-conference support is essential to reinforce agreements, promote ongoing healing, and prevent recidivism. Continuous monitoring and emotional support help sustain the positive outcomes of the restorative process.

Challenges and Solutions

Common Challenges

Restorative justice faces challenges such as resistance from participants, power imbalances, and safety concerns.

Recognizing and addressing these challenges is crucial for effective implementation.

Solutions and Best Practices

Strategies to overcome challenges include building trust and rapport, providing education and support, ensuring safety, and maintaining high standards for facilitation. These best practices enhance the effectiveness of restorative justice.

Policy and Legal Considerations

Supportive Legal Frameworks

Legal and policy frameworks play a significant role in supporting or hindering restorative justice. Advocacy for legislative support and the integration of restorative practices into the justice system are key to expanding its reach.

Addressing Barriers

Challenges such as lack of legal recognition and confidentiality concerns can be addressed through targeted advocacy, policy development, and training for legal professionals.

Expanding Applications

Restorative Justice in Various Contexts

Restorative justice can be applied in schools, workplaces, and communities, addressing conflicts, promoting healing, and fostering positive change across different settings.

Addressing Systemic Issues

Restorative justice has the potential to address systemic issues such as inequality and social justice by providing a platform for marginalized voices and promoting equitable solutions.

Vision for the Future

Transforming the Justice System

The future vision for restorative justice includes its widespread adoption within the mainstream justice system, the establishment of restorative justice courts, and comprehensive training for justice professionals.

Influencing Societal Values

Promoting empathy, understanding, and community engagement can lead to a cultural shift towards a more restorative society. Integrating restorative principles into education and public awareness campaigns can further this vision.

Driving Systemic Change

Restorative justice can address the root causes of crime and promote systemic changes that support a more just and equitable society. Global collaboration and policy advocacy are crucial for advancing this transformative approach.

Implications for Families and Communities

Restorative justice offers significant benefits for families and communities. By addressing harm, promoting healing, and fostering accountability, restorative justice strengthens relationships and builds resilient, supportive communities. As restorative practices continue to evolve and expand, their potential to transform the justice system and society becomes increasingly evident.

Conclusion

This book has explored the multifaceted impact of restorative justice on families, communities, and the justice system. By emphasizing healing, accountability, and community engagement, restorative justice provides a powerful framework for addressing crime and conflict. As we look to the future, continued innovation, collaboration, and advocacy for restorative justice will be essential in realizing its transformative potential.

Call to Action

Restorative justice has the potential to transform lives, families, communities, and entire justice systems. However, this transformation requires active participation and advocacy from individuals, communities, and institutions. This chapter encourages readers to take action by advocating for and participating in restorative justice practices to foster healing and reconciliation.

Understanding Your Role in Restorative Justice

Individual Responsibility

1. Educate Yourself: Learn about restorative justice principles and practices. Understanding how restorative justice works is the first step in becoming an effective advocate and participant.

2. Reflect on Personal Experiences: Consider how restorative justice principles might apply to conflicts or harms you have experienced or witnessed. Reflect on how these principles could facilitate healing and resolution.

3. Practice Empathy and Accountability: In your daily interactions, practice empathy, active listening, and accountability. These skills are foundational to restorative justice and can transform personal and professional relationships.

Community Engagement

1. Promote Awareness: Share information about restorative justice with your community. Host discussions, workshops, or book clubs to spread awareness and educate others.

2. Support Local Initiatives: Get involved with local organizations that offer restorative justice programs. Volunteer your time, donate resources, or help organize events to support these initiatives.

3. Build Restorative Communities: Encourage schools, workplaces, and community organizations to adopt restorative justice practices. Advocate for the integration of restorative approaches into existing conflict resolution processes.

Advocacy for Restorative Justice

Policy Advocacy

1. Engage with Policymakers: Reach out to local, state, and national policymakers to advocate for restorative justice legislation. Share success stories and data that highlight the effectiveness of restorative justice practices.

2. Support Legislative Efforts: Support bills and policies that promote restorative justice by writing letters, signing petitions, and participating in advocacy campaigns.

3. Collaborate with Advocacy Groups: Join or collaborate with advocacy groups that are working to advance restorative justice. These groups often have the resources and networks to amplify your advocacy efforts.

Legal and Educational Reforms

1. Integrate Restorative Practices in Education: Advocate for the inclusion of restorative justice principles in school curricula and disciplinary processes. Support restorative justice training for educators and administrators.

2. Promote Legal Training: Encourage law schools and legal training programs to include restorative justice in their curricula. Advocate for continuing education on restorative practices for legal professionals.

3. Support Research and Evaluation: Advocate for research and evaluation of restorative justice programs to build a robust evidence base. Support academic and community-based research initiatives that explore the impacts and best practices of restorative justice.

Participating in Restorative Justice Practices

Becoming a Facilitator

1. Seek Training: If you are interested in becoming a restorative justice facilitator, seek out training programs that offer comprehensive education on restorative practices. Certification programs are available through various organizations and institutions.

2. Gain Experience: Volunteer with local restorative justice programs to gain practical experience. Observing and co-facilitating with experienced practitioners can help you develop your skills.

3. Commit to Continuous Learning: Restorative justice is an evolving field. Commit to ongoing learning and professional development to stay informed about new practices, research, and innovations.

Participating as a Community Member

1. Join Restorative Circles: Participate in restorative circles in your community. Whether as a victim, offender, or community member, your involvement can help foster healing and reconciliation.

2. Support Restorative Initiatives: Attend events, fundraisers, and awareness campaigns organized by restorative justice organizations. Your support can help sustain and expand these initiatives.

3. Provide Feedback: Offer constructive feedback to restorative justice programs to help them improve and adapt. Sharing your experiences and perspectives can contribute to the growth and effectiveness of restorative practices.

Inspiring Others

Sharing Stories

1. Personal Testimonials: Share your personal experiences with restorative justice to inspire others. Personal stories can be powerful tools for illustrating the impact of restorative practices.

2. Highlighting Successes: Share success stories from your community or from around the world. Highlighting the positive outcomes of restorative justice can encourage others to get involved.

3. Creating Platforms: Use social media, blogs, podcasts, and other platforms to spread the message of restorative justice. Create content that educates, informs, and inspires action.

Building Networks

1. Connecting with Like-Minded Individuals: Build networks with others who are passionate about restorative justice. Collaborate on projects, share resources, and support each other's efforts.

2. Mentorship: Mentor others who are interested in restorative justice. Share your knowledge and experience to help them become effective advocates and practitioners.

3. Community Leadership: Take on leadership roles within your community to promote restorative justice. Lead by example and inspire others to join you in creating a more just and compassionate society.

Conclusion

The potential of restorative justice to transform the justice system and society is immense, but realizing this potential requires collective action. By educating ourselves, engaging with our communities, advocating for policy and legal reforms, and actively participating in restorative practices, we can foster healing, reconciliation, and a more just world.

This call to action is an invitation to become part of the restorative justice movement. Whether you are a victim seeking healing, an offender seeking redemption, or a community member seeking justice, your involvement matters. Together, we can create a future where restorative justice is not just an alternative but the standard approach to addressing harm and conflict. Let us embrace this vision and work towards a more restorative and compassionate world.

APPENDICES

RESOURCES FOR PRACTITIONERS

Restorative justice practitioners can benefit from a wealth of resources, including organizations, training programs, literature, and online platforms. This chapter provides a comprehensive list of resources to support practitioners in their work, offering tools for education, professional development, and community engagement.

Organizations

National and International Organizations

1. Restorative Justice International (RJI): A global association that promotes restorative justice practices worldwide. RJI offers resources, networking opportunities, and advocacy tools.

- Website: [restorativejusticeinternational.com](http://www.restorativejusticeinternational.com)

2. International Institute for Restorative Practices (IIRP): An educational institution dedicated to the study and promotion of restorative practices. IIRP provides training, conferences, and publications.

- Website: [iirp.edu](http://www.iirp.edu)

3. European Forum for Restorative Justice (EFRJ): An organization that supports the development of restorative justice in Europe through research, policy advocacy, and practice.

- Website: [euforumrj.org](http://www.euforumrj.org)

4. National Association of Community and Restorative Justice (NACRJ): An American organization that fosters community and restorative justice practices through education, training, and networking.

- Website: [nacrj.org](http://www.nacrj.org)

5. The Centre for Justice & Reconciliation: A program of Prison Fellowship International that promotes restorative justice principles and practices globally.

- Website: [restorativejustice.org](http://www.restorativejustice.org)

Regional and Local Organizations

1. Restorative Justice Council (RJC): Based in the UK, RJC sets standards for restorative justice practices and provides accreditation, training, and resources.

- Website: [restorativejustice.org.uk](http://www.restorativejustice.org.uk)

2. Community Justice Initiatives (CJI): A Canadian organization that develops and delivers restorative justice programs and services.

- Website: [cjiwr.com](http://www.cjiwr.com)

3. Transformative Justice Australia: An organization that provides training, consultancy, and resources for restorative and transformative justice practices.

- Website: [transformativejusticeaustralia.com.au](http://www.transformativejusticeaustralia.com.au)

4. Restorative Justice for Oakland Youth (RJOY): A local organization in Oakland, California, dedicated to implementing restorative justice practices in schools and communities.

- Website: [rjoyoakland.org](http://www.rjoyoakland.org)

Training Programs

1. IIRP Training Programs: The International Institute for Restorative Practices offers a variety of training programs, including professional development courses, certifications, and graduate programs.

- Website: [iirp.edu/training](http://www.iirp.edu/training)

2. Restorative Justice Academy: An online platform offering courses and certifications in restorative justice practices for educators, justice professionals, and community leaders.

- Website: [restorativejusticeacademy.com](http://www.restorativejusticeacademy.com)

3. Peacemaking Circles Training: Provided by the Center for Restorative Justice & Peacemaking, this training focuses on the use of peacemaking circles in various contexts.

- Website: [rjp.umn.edu](http://www.rjp.umn.edu)

4. RJC Accredited Training: The Restorative Justice Council in the UK offers accredited training programs for practitioners, including facilitator training and advanced courses.

- Website: [restorativejustice.org.uk/learning-and-development](http://www.restorativejustice.org.uk/learning-and-development)

5. Community Works West Training: Based in California, Community Works West offers training programs on restorative justice practices, particularly in school and community settings.

- Website: [communityworkswest.org](http://www.communityworkswest.org)

Literature

Foundational Texts

1. "The Little Book of Restorative Justice" by Howard Zehr: A seminal text that introduces the principles and practices of restorative justice.

- ISBN: 978-1561488230

2. "Restorative Justice: Ideas, Values, Debates" by Gerry Johnstone: An in-depth exploration of the concepts and debates surrounding restorative justice.

- ISBN: 978-1138805654

3. "Changing Lenses: Restorative Justice for Our Times" by Howard Zehr: A comprehensive examination of restorative justice and its potential to transform the justice system.

- ISBN: 978-0836199477

Practical Guides

1. "The Little Book of Circle Processes: A New/Old Approach to Peacemaking" by Kay Pranis: A practical guide to using circle processes in restorative justice.

- ISBN: 978-1561484614

2. "Restorative Circles in Schools: Building Community and Enhancing Learning" by Bob Costello, Joshua Wachtel, and Ted Wachtel: A guide to implementing restorative circles in educational settings.

- ISBN: 978-1934355040

3. "The Little Book of Family Group Conferences New Zealand Style" by Allan MacRae and Howard Zehr: A practical resource on using family group conferences in restorative justice.

- ISBN: 978-1561485062

Advanced Readings

1. "Restorative Justice: Theories and Practices of Moral Imagination" edited by Theo Gavrielides: A collection of essays exploring advanced theoretical and practical aspects of restorative justice.

- ISBN: 978-1904303876

2. "Restorative Justice Today: Practical Applications" edited by Katherine S. Van Wormer and Lorenn Walker: A compilation of case studies and practical applications of restorative justice in various contexts.

- ISBN: 978-1483317458

3. "The Handbook of Restorative Justice" edited by Dennis Sullivan and Larry Tifft: An extensive reference book covering a wide range of topics related to restorative justice.

- ISBN: 978-0415439945

Online Platforms and Resources

1. Restorative Justice Online: A comprehensive resource offering articles, case studies, and tools for practitioners.

- Website: [restorativejustice.org](http://www.restorativejustice.org)

2. Restorative Justice Network: An online community for restorative justice practitioners to share resources, experiences, and best practices.

- Website: [rjnetwork.org](http://www.rjnetwork.org)

3. RJ Library: An extensive digital library of restorative justice literature, including research papers, books, and articles.

- Website: [rjlibrary.org](http://www.rjlibrary.org)

4. Transform Harm: A resource hub providing information, tools, and resources on transformative justice and community-based approaches to addressing harm.

- Website: [transformharm.org](http://www.transformharm.org)

5. Center for Restorative Justice at Suffolk University: Offers resources, training, and research on restorative justice practices.

- Website: [suffolk.edu/academics/research-at-suffolk/center-for-restorative-justice](http://www.suffolk.edu/academics/research-at-suffolk/center-for-restorative-justice)

Conclusion

This comprehensive list of resources provides a solid foundation for restorative justice practitioners to enhance their knowledge, skills, and impact. By leveraging these organizations, training programs, literature, and online platforms, practitioners can continue to grow and contribute to the transformative power of restorative justice. The future of restorative justice depends on the dedication and collaboration of individuals and communities committed to fostering healing, accountability, and reconciliation.

APPENDICES

SAMPLE CONFERENCE SCRIPTS

Conducting restorative justice conferences requires careful preparation and structured facilitation to ensure a safe and productive process. This chapter provides sample scripts and guidelines for different types of restorative justice conferences, including victim-offender mediation, family group conferencing, and community conferencing. These scripts serve as a reference for facilitators to guide the process, foster open dialogue, and promote healing and accountability.

Sample Script for Victim-Offender Mediation

Introduction and Ground Rules

Facilitator: "Welcome, everyone. My name is [Facilitator's Name], and I will be facilitating this mediation session. The purpose of our meeting today is to discuss the harm caused by the incident, understand each other's perspectives, and work toward a resolution that promotes healing and accountability. Before we begin, let's establish some ground rules to ensure a respectful and productive conversation."

Facilitator: "First, we will speak one at a time. Please wait for your turn to speak and listen attentively to others. Second, we will speak respectfully and avoid any blame or accusations. Third, everything discussed here will remain confidential. Does everyone agree to these ground rules?"

Participants: (Nod or verbally agree)

Opening Statements

Facilitator: "Let's start with opening statements. [Victim's Name], please share your experience of what happened and how it has affected you."

Victim: (Shares their experience and the impact of the incident)

Facilitator: "Thank you, [Victim's Name]. [Offender's Name], please share your perspective on what happened and how you feel about it now."

Offender: (Shares their perspective and feelings)

Facilitated Dialogue

Facilitator: "Now that we have heard both perspectives, let's discuss the incident in more detail. [Victim's

Name], can you tell us more about how this incident has affected your life?"

Victim: (Provides additional details and impact)

Facilitator: "[Offender's Name], how do you feel hearing [Victim's Name]'s experience? What are your thoughts?"

Offender: (Responds with thoughts and feelings)

Facilitator: "What steps do you think you can take to address the harm caused and make amends?"

Offender: (Offers suggestions for reparation)

Facilitator: "[Victim's Name], how do you feel about [Offender's Name]'s suggestions? Is there anything else you would like to see happen?"

Victim: (Provides feedback and additional requests)

Developing a Resolution Plan

Facilitator: "Let's work together to create a resolution plan that addresses the harm and promotes healing. [Offender's Name], based on our discussion, what commitments are you willing to make?"

Offender: (Lists commitments)

Facilitator: "[Victim's Name], do these commitments meet your needs? Is there anything you would like to add or change?"

Victim: (Agrees or suggests modifications)

Facilitator: "Great. Let's summarize the resolution plan. [Offender's Name] will [list of commitments], and [Victim's Name] will [list of any agreed support or actions]. Does everyone agree to this plan?"

Participants: (Agree to the plan)

Closing the Session

Facilitator: "Thank you both for your participation and willingness to work towards resolution. This concludes our session. We will schedule a follow-up meeting to review the progress of the resolution plan. Please reach out if you have any concerns or need support before then."

Sample Script for Family Group Conferencing

Introduction and Ground Rules

Facilitator: "Welcome, everyone. My name is [Facilitator's Name], and I will be facilitating this family group conference. Our goal today is to discuss the incident, understand its impact on the family, and develop a plan to address the harm and support each other moving forward. Let's start by establishing some ground rules to ensure a respectful and productive discussion."

Facilitator: "First, we will speak one at a time and listen without interrupting. Second, we will speak respectfully and avoid blaming or accusing each other. Third, everything discussed here will remain confidential. Does everyone agree to these ground rules?"

Participants: (Nod or verbally agree)

Opening Statements

Facilitator: "Let's begin with opening statements. [Victim's Name], please share your experience of the incident and how it has affected you."

Victim: (Shares their experience and the impact of the incident)

Facilitator: "Thank you, [Victim's Name]. [Offender's Name], please share your perspective on what happened and how you feel about it now."

Offender: (Shares their perspective and feelings)

Facilitator: "Now, let's hear from other family members. [Family Member's Name], please share how this incident has affected you and your thoughts on the situation."

Family Member: (Shares their experience and thoughts)

Facilitated Dialogue

Facilitator: "Now that we have heard from everyone, let's discuss the incident in more detail. [Victim's Name], can you tell us more about how this incident has affected your daily life and relationships within the family?"

Victim: (Provides additional details and impact)

Facilitator: "[Offender's Name], how do you feel hearing [Victim's Name]'s experience? What are your thoughts?"

Offender: (Responds with thoughts and feelings)

Facilitator: "Other family members, how do you feel about what has been shared so far? What are your thoughts on how we can move forward as a family?"

Family Members: (Share their thoughts and feelings)

Developing a Family Plan

Facilitator: "Let's work together to create a family plan that addresses the harm and promotes healing and support. [Offender's Name], based on our discussion, what steps are you willing to take to address the harm caused?"

Offender: (Lists commitments)

Facilitator: "[Victim's Name], do these commitments meet your needs? Is there anything else you would like to add or change?"

Victim: (Provides feedback and additional requests)

Facilitator: "Family members, what additional steps can we take as a family to support each other and ensure this doesn't happen again?"

Family Members: (Offer suggestions and commitments)

Facilitator: "Let's summarize the family plan. [Offender's Name] will [list of commitments], [Victim's Name] will [list of agreed support or actions], and the family will [list of collective commitments]. Does everyone agree to this plan?"

Participants: (Agree to the plan)

Closing the Session

Facilitator: "Thank you all for your participation and willingness to work towards resolution as a family. This concludes our session. We will schedule a follow-up meeting to review the progress of the family plan. Please reach out if you have any concerns or need support before then."

Sample Script for Community Conferencing

Introduction and Ground Rules

Facilitator: "Welcome, everyone. My name is [Facilitator's Name], and I will be facilitating this community conference. Our goal today is to discuss the incident that has affected our community, understand its impact, and develop a plan to address the harm and strengthen our community bonds. Let's start by establishing some ground rules to ensure a respectful and productive discussion."

Facilitator: "First, we will speak one at a time and listen without interrupting. Second, we will speak respectfully and avoid blaming or accusing each other. Third, everything discussed here will remain confidential. Does everyone agree to these ground rules?"

Participants: (Nod or verbally agree)

Opening Statements

Facilitator: "Let's begin with opening statements. [Victim's Name], please share your experience of the incident and how it has affected you."

Victim: (Shares their experience and the impact of the incident)

Facilitator: "Thank you, [Victim's Name]. [Offender's Name], please share your perspective on what happened and how you feel about it now."

Offender: (Shares their perspective and feelings)

Facilitator: "Now, let's hear from other community members. [Community Member's Name], please share how this incident has affected you and your thoughts on the situation."

Community Member: (Shares their experience and thoughts)

Facilitated Dialogue

Facilitator: "Now that we have heard from everyone, let's discuss the incident in more detail. [Victim's Name], can you tell us more about how this incident has affected your daily life and your sense of safety in the community?"

Victim: (Provides additional details and impact)

Facilitator: "[Offender's Name], how do you feel hearing [Victim's Name]'s experience? What are your thoughts?"

Offender: (Responds with thoughts and feelings)

Facilitator: "Other community members, how do you feel about what has been shared so far? What are your thoughts on how we can move forward as a community?"

Community Members: (Share their thoughts and feelings)

Developing a Community Plan

Facilitator: "Let's work together to create a community plan that addresses the harm and promotes healing and support. [Offender's Name], based on our discussion, what steps are you willing to take to address the harm caused?"

Offender: (Lists commitments)

Facilitator

: "[Victim's Name], do these commitments meet your needs? Is there anything else you would like to add or change?"

Victim: (Provides feedback and additional requests)

Facilitator: "Community members, what additional steps can we take as a community to support each other and ensure this doesn't happen again?"

Community Members: (Offer suggestions and commitments)

Facilitator: "Let's summarize the community plan. [Offender's Name] will [list of commitments], [Victim's Name] will [list of agreed support or actions], and the community will [list of collective commitments]. Does everyone agree to this plan?"

Participants: (Agree to the plan)

Closing the Session

Facilitator: "Thank you all for your participation and willingness to work towards resolution as a community. This concludes our session. We will schedule a follow-up meeting to review the progress of the community plan. Please reach out if you have any concerns or need support before then."

Conclusion

These sample scripts provide a framework for conducting various types of restorative justice conferences. While each conference will vary based on the specific context and participants, these scripts offer a starting point for facilitators to guide the process effectively. By fostering open dialogue, empathy, and accountability, restorative justice conferences can promote healing and reconciliation within families, communities, and beyond.

APPENDICES

ADDITIONAL CASE STUDIES

To further illustrate the diversity and impact of restorative justice conferencing, this chapter presents additional case studies. These examples highlight the versatility of restorative justice in different contexts, demonstrating its effectiveness in addressing various types of harm and fostering healing and reconciliation.

Case Study 1: School Bullying Incident

Background

In a middle school, a series of bullying incidents occurred involving a group of students targeting a classmate, Sarah. The bullying included verbal harassment, spreading rumors, and social exclusion. Sarah's parents reported the incidents to the school administration, which decided to implement a restorative justice conference to address the issue.

The Conference

Participants: Sarah (victim), the group of students involved in the bullying (offenders), their parents, and school staff.

Facilitator's Role: The facilitator began by setting ground rules and explaining the purpose of the conference. Each participant was given the opportunity to share their perspective.

Victim's Perspective: Sarah described how the bullying had affected her self-esteem, her ability to concentrate in class, and her overall well-being. She expressed feelings of fear and sadness and the desire for the bullying to stop.

Offenders' Perspective: The group of students acknowledged their actions, though some were initially defensive. Through facilitated dialogue, they began to understand the impact of their behavior on Sarah. They expressed regret and apologized.

Family and Staff Perspectives: Parents and school staff shared their concerns about the impact of bullying on all students and the school environment. They emphasized the importance of creating a supportive and inclusive atmosphere.

Resolution Plan

The resolution plan included commitments from the offending students to stop the bullying, participate in empathy-building activities, and engage in a peer support group. Sarah received ongoing counseling support, and the school implemented anti-bullying workshops for all students.

Outcome

The bullying incidents stopped, and the school environment improved. Sarah reported feeling safer and more supported. The offending students learned about the impact of their behavior and developed better interpersonal skills. The school's proactive approach strengthened the community and reinforced a culture of respect and inclusion.

Case Study 2: Workplace Conflict

Background

In a corporate office, a conflict arose between two employees, John and Lisa, over project responsibilities. The conflict escalated to the point where it affected team morale and productivity. The human resources department decided to use a restorative justice conference to resolve the issue.

The Conference

Participants: John (employee), Lisa (employee), their immediate supervisor, and a representative from human resources.

Facilitator's Role: The facilitator established ground rules and explained the restorative justice process. Each participant was invited to share their experience and perspective on the conflict.

John's Perspective: John felt that Lisa was undermining his contributions and taking credit for his work. He expressed frustration and a sense of being undervalued.

Lisa's Perspective: Lisa felt that John was not collaborating effectively and was resistant to feedback. She expressed concerns about project deadlines and team dynamics.

Supervisor's Perspective: The supervisor emphasized the importance of collaboration and effective communication for the team's success. They expressed a desire to see both employees work together harmoniously.

Resolution Plan

The resolution plan included commitments from John and Lisa to improve their communication, clarify their roles and responsibilities, and participate in a team-building workshop. The supervisor agreed to provide ongoing support and mediation if needed.

Outcome

John and Lisa's working relationship improved, leading to better collaboration and increased productivity.

The team-building workshop strengthened the overall team dynamic. The human resources department recognized the value of restorative justice in resolving workplace conflicts and considered implementing it more broadly.

Case Study 3: Community Vandalism

Background

In a small town, a group of teenagers vandalized a local park, causing significant damage to public property. The community was outraged, and there were calls for severe punishment. The local council decided to hold a restorative justice conference to address the incident.

The Conference

Participants: The teenagers (offenders), their parents, community members, and representatives from the local council.

Facilitator's Role: The facilitator opened the session by setting ground rules and explaining the purpose of the conference. Each participant was invited to share their perspective.

Community Members' Perspective: Community members expressed their disappointment and anger over the vandalism. They highlighted the importance of the park as a community space and the impact of the damage on the town's spirit.

Offenders' Perspective: The teenagers admitted to the vandalism, explaining that they acted out of boredom and peer pressure. They expressed regret and apologized to the community.

Parent's Perspective: The parents shared their concerns about their children's actions and their willingness to support efforts to make amends.

Resolution Plan

The resolution plan included commitments from the teenagers to repair the damage they caused, participate in community service projects, and attend a workshop on civic responsibility. The local council agreed to support the rehabilitation efforts and provide resources for the repair work.

Outcome

The teenagers repaired the damage to the park, and their participation in community service projects helped them build a sense of responsibility and connection to their community. The community appreciated the effort to make amends and welcomed the teenagers back with understanding and support. The restorative justice process strengthened community bonds and reinforced the value of civic engagement.

Case Study 4: Domestic Violence

Background

A domestic violence incident occurred between a couple, Maria and David. David had physically assaulted Maria during an argument, leading to his arrest. After seeking help from a local support organization, Maria expressed a desire for a restorative justice conference to address the harm and seek a resolution.

The Conference

Participants: Maria (victim), David (offender), their respective support persons, and a representative from the support organization.

Facilitator's Role: The facilitator set ground rules and ensured a safe environment for the discussion. Each participant was given the opportunity to share their experience and perspective.

Maria's Perspective: Maria described the emotional and physical impact of the violence on her and expressed her need for safety and assurance that the behavior would not be repeated.

David's Perspective: David admitted to his actions, expressed deep regret, and acknowledged the harm he caused. He shared his commitment to seeking help for anger management and changing his behavior.

Support Persons' Perspective: The support persons provided additional context, emphasizing the importance of addressing the root causes of the violence and ensuring Maria's safety.

Resolution Plan

The resolution plan included commitments from David to attend anger management counseling, participate in a domestic violence intervention program, and avoid any further contact with Maria until she felt safe. Maria received ongoing support from the organization, including counseling and safety planning.

Outcome

David adhered to the resolution plan, actively participating in counseling and intervention programs. Maria felt safer and supported, and her emotional well-being improved. The restorative justice conference provided a platform for accountability and healing, demonstrating the potential of restorative justice in addressing complex and sensitive issues.

Conclusion

These additional case studies illustrate the diverse applications and significant impact of restorative justice conferencing in various contexts. From school bullying and workplace conflicts to community vandalism and domestic violence, restorative justice provides a framework for addressing harm, promoting healing, and fostering accountability. These examples highlight the versatility and effectiveness of restorative justice practices, offering valuable insights for practitioners and communities committed to creating a more just and compassionate society.

COMPREHENSIVE BIBLIOGRAPHY

This comprehensive bibliography lists all the sources cited in the book, providing readers with further reading and research opportunities. These references cover a wide range of topics related to restorative justice, including theoretical foundations, practical applications, case studies, and policy considerations.

Books

1. Zehr, H. (2002). "The Little Book of Restorative Justice." Good Books.

- A seminal text introducing the principles and practices of restorative justice.

2. Johnstone, G. (2013). "Restorative Justice: Ideas, Values, Debates." Routledge.

- An in-depth exploration of the concepts and debates surrounding restorative justice.

3. Zehr, H. (2005). "Changing Lenses: Restorative Justice for Our Times." Herald Press.

- A comprehensive examination of restorative justice and its potential to transform the justice system.

4. Pranis, K. (2005). "The Little Book of Circle Processes: A New/Old Approach to Peacemaking." Good Books.

- A practical guide to using circle processes in restorative justice.

5. Costello, B., Wachtel, J., & Wachtel, T. (2009). "Restorative Circles in Schools: Building Community and Enhancing Learning." IIRP.

- A guide to implementing restorative circles in educational settings.

6. MacRae, A., & Zehr, H. (2004). "The Little Book of Family Group Conferences New Zealand Style." Good Books.

- A practical resource on using family group conferences in restorative justice.

7. Gavrielides, T. (Ed.). (2007). "Restorative Justice: Theories and Practices of Moral Imagination." Interchange.

- A collection of essays exploring advanced theoretical and practical aspects of restorative justice.

8. Van Wormer, K. S., & Walker, L. (Eds.). (2013). "Restorative Justice Today: Practical Applications." SAGE Publications.

- A compilation of case studies and practical applications of restorative justice in various contexts.

9. Sullivan, D., & Tifft, L. (Eds.). (2006). "The Handbook of Restorative Justice." Routledge.

- An extensive reference book covering a wide range of topics related to restorative justice.

Articles and Papers

1. Bazemore, G., & Schiff, M. (2005). "Juvenile Justice Reform and Restorative Justice: Building Theory and Policy from Practice." Willan Publishing.

- An article discussing the integration of restorative justice principles into juvenile justice reform.

2. Braithwaite, J. (2002). "Restorative Justice & Responsive Regulation." Oxford University Press.

- A paper exploring the relationship between restorative justice and regulatory frameworks.

3. Daly, K. (2006). "The Limits of Restorative Justice." In D. Sullivan & L. Tifft (Eds.), "The Handbook of Restorative Justice" (pp. 134-145). Routledge.

- A critical examination of the limitations and challenges of restorative justice.

4. Johnstone, G., & Van Ness, D. W. (2007). "Handbook of Restorative Justice." Willan Publishing.

- A comprehensive overview of restorative justice theories, practices, and debates.

5. Zehr, H., & Mika, H. (1998). "Fundamental Concepts of Restorative Justice." Contemporary Justice Review, 1(1), 47-55.

- An article outlining the fundamental concepts and principles of restorative justice.

Reports and Guidelines

1. Restorative Justice Council. (2011). "Best Practice Guidance for Restorative Practice."

- A report providing guidelines and best practices for implementing restorative justice.

2. International Institute for Restorative Practices. (2009). "Restorative Justice: The Evidence."

- A comprehensive review of the evidence supporting the effectiveness of restorative justice practices.

3. United Nations Office on Drugs and Crime. (2006). "Handbook on Restorative Justice Programmes."

- A guide for practitioners and policymakers on implementing restorative justice programs.

4. Ministry of Justice, New Zealand. (2011). "Restorative Justice in New Zealand: Best Practice Framework."

- A framework outlining best practices for restorative justice in New Zealand.

Websites and Online Resources

1. Restorative Justice International. [restorativejusticeinternational.com](http://www.restorativejusticeinternational.com)

- A global association promoting restorative justice practices worldwide.

2. International Institute for Restorative Practices. [iirp.edu](http://www.iirp.edu)

- An educational institution dedicated to the study and promotion of restorative practices.

3. European Forum for Restorative Justice. [euforumrj.org](http://www.euforumrj.org)

- An organization supporting the development of restorative justice in Europe.

4. National Association of Community and Restorative Justice. [nacrj.org](http://www.nacrj.org)

- An American organization fostering community and restorative justice practices.

5. The Centre for Justice & Reconciliation. [restorativejustice.org](http://www.restorativejustice.org)

- A program promoting restorative justice principles and practices globally.

6. Restorative Justice Council. [restorativejustice.org.uk](http://www.restorativejustice.org.uk)

- A UK-based organization providing standards, accreditation, and resources for restorative justice.

7. Community Justice Initiatives. [cjiwr.com](http://www.cjiwr.com)

- A Canadian organization developing and delivering restorative justice programs.

8. Transformative Justice Australia. [transformativejusticeaustralia.com.au](http://www.transformativejusticeaustralia.com.au)

- An organization providing training, consultancy, and resources for restorative and transformative justice.

9. Restorative Justice for Oakland Youth. [rjoyoakland.org](http://www.rjoyoakland.org)

- A local organization in Oakland, California, implementing restorative justice practices in schools and communities.

10. Restorative Justice Academy. [restorativejusticeacademy.com](http://www.restorativejusticeacademy.com)

- An online platform offering courses and certifications in restorative justice practices.

11. Peacemaking Circles Training. [rjp.umn.edu](http://www.rjp.umn.edu)

- Training provided by the Center for Restorative Justice & Peacemaking on the use of peacemaking circles.

12. Community Works West. [communityworkswest.org](http://www.communityworkswest.org)

- An organization offering restorative justice training and programs in California.

13. Restorative Justice Online. [restorativejustice.org](http://www.restorativejustice.org)

- A comprehensive online resource offering articles, case studies, and tools for restorative justice practitioners.

14. Restorative Justice Network. [rjnetwork.org](http://www.rjnetwork.org)

- An online community for restorative justice practitioners to share resources, experiences, and best practices.

15. RJ Library. [rjlibrary.org](http://www.rjlibrary.org)

- A digital library of restorative justice literature, including research papers, books, and articles.

16. Transform Harm. [transformharm.org](http://www.transformharm.org)

- A resource hub providing information, tools, and resources on transformative justice and community-based approaches.

17. Center for Restorative Justice at Suffolk University. [suffolk.edu/academics/research-at-suffolk/center-for-restorative-justice](http://www.suffolk.edu/academics/research-at-suffolk/center-for-restorative-justice)

- Offers resources, training, and research on restorative justice practices.

Conclusion

This comprehensive bibliography provides a wide range of resources for further reading and research on restorative justice. By exploring these sources, readers can deepen their understanding of restorative justice principles and practices, enhance their professional skills, and contribute to the ongoing development of restorative justice as a transformative approach to addressing harm and conflict.

APPENDICES

SUGGESTED READING

For readers interested in delving deeper into restorative justice and family reunification, this chapter provides a curated list of additional books and articles. These recommended readings offer a variety of perspectives, case studies, and practical insights into restorative justice practices and their applications in different contexts.

Foundational Texts

1. "The Little Book of Restorative Justice" by Howard Zehr

- A seminal text introducing the principles and practices of restorative justice, making it accessible for both new and experienced practitioners.

- ISBN: 978-1561488230

2. "Restorative Justice: Ideas, Values, Debates" by Gerry Johnstone

- An in-depth exploration of the concepts and debates surrounding restorative justice, providing a comprehensive understanding of its theoretical foundations.

- ISBN: 978-1138805654

3. "Changing Lenses: Restorative Justice for Our Times" by Howard Zehr

- A comprehensive examination of restorative justice and its potential to transform the justice system, with a focus on changing perspectives from retribution to restoration.

- ISBN: 978-0836199477

Practical Guides

1. "The Little Book of Circle Processes: A New/Old Approach to Peacemaking" by Kay Pranis

- A practical guide to using circle processes in restorative justice, offering step-by-step instructions and case examples.

- ISBN: 978-1561484614

2. "Restorative Circles in Schools: Building Community and Enhancing Learning" by Bob Costello, Joshua Wachtel, and Ted Wachtel

- A guide to implementing restorative circles in educational settings, focusing on building community and enhancing learning outcomes.

- ISBN: 978-1934355040

3. "The Little Book of Family Group Conferences New Zealand Style" by Allan MacRae and Howard Zehr

- A practical resource on using family group conferences in restorative justice, drawing on the New Zealand model.

- ISBN: 978-1561485062

Advanced Readings

1. "Restorative Justice: Theories and Practices of Moral Imagination" edited by Theo Gavrielides

- A collection of essays exploring advanced theoretical and practical aspects of restorative justice, suitable for scholars and advanced practitioners.

- ISBN: 978-1904303876

2. "Restorative Justice Today: Practical Applications" edited by Katherine S. Van Wormer and Lorenn Walker

- A compilation of case studies and practical applications of restorative justice in various contexts, highlighting contemporary practices and innovations.

- ISBN: 978-1483317458

3. "The Handbook of Restorative Justice" edited by Dennis Sullivan and Larry Tifft

- An extensive reference book covering a wide range of topics related to restorative justice, from theoretical frameworks to practical implementations.
- ISBN: 978-0415439945

Articles and Papers

1. Bazemore, G., & Schiff, M. (2005). "Juvenile Justice Reform and Restorative Justice: Building Theory and Policy from Practice." Willan Publishing.

- Discusses the integration of restorative justice principles into juvenile justice reform, providing theoretical and policy insights.

2. Braithwaite, J. (2002). "Restorative Justice & Responsive Regulation." Oxford University Press.

- Explores the relationship between restorative justice and regulatory frameworks, offering a comprehensive analysis of their interplay.

3. Daly, K. (2006). "The Limits of Restorative Justice." In D. Sullivan & L. Tifft (Eds.), "The Handbook of Restorative Justice" (pp. 134-145). Routledge.

- A critical examination of the limitations and challenges of restorative justice, providing a balanced view of its potential and constraints.

4. Zehr, H., & Mika, H. (1998). "Fundamental Concepts of Restorative Justice." Contemporary Justice Review, 1(1), 47-55.

- An article outlining the fundamental concepts and principles of restorative justice, suitable for both newcomers and seasoned practitioners.

5. Johnstone, G., & Van Ness, D. W. (2007). "Handbook of Restorative Justice." Willan Publishing.

- Provides a comprehensive overview of restorative justice theories, practices, and debates, suitable for academic and professional audiences.

Specialized Topics

1. "Restorative Justice and Family Violence" edited by Heather Strang and John Braithwaite

- Explores the application of restorative justice in cases of family violence, discussing its challenges and potential benefits.

- ISBN: 978-0521521659

2. "Conferencing and Restorative Justice: International Practices and Perspectives" edited by Estelle Zinsstag and Inge Vanfraechem

- Analyzes the use of conferencing in restorative justice across different international contexts, offering comparative insights.

- ISBN: 978-0199655038

3. "Victims and Restorative Justice" by Inge Vanfraechem, Antony Pemberton, and Felix Mukwiza Ndahinda

- Focuses on the role and experiences of victims in restorative justice processes, providing a victim-centered perspective.

- ISBN: 978-0415708249

Online Resources

1. Restorative Justice International

- A global association promoting restorative justice practices worldwide, offering a wealth of resources and networking opportunities.

- Website: [restorativejusticeinternational.com](http://www.restorativejusticeinternational.com)

2. International Institute for Restorative Practices

- An educational institution dedicated to the study and promotion of restorative practices, providing training and publications.

- Website: [iirp.edu](http://www.iirp.edu)

3. Restorative Justice Council

- A UK-based organization providing standards, accreditation, and resources for restorative justice.

- Website: [restorativejustice.org.uk](http://www.restorativejustice.org.uk)

4. Center for Restorative Justice at Suffolk University

- Offers resources, training, and research on restorative justice practices, suitable for practitioners and scholars.

- Website: [suffolk.edu/academics/research-at-suffolk/center-for-restorative-justice](http://www.suffolk.edu/academics/research-at-suffolk/center-for-restorative-justice)

5. Restorative Justice Online

- A comprehensive online resource offering articles, case studies, and tools for restorative justice practitioners.

- Website: [restorativejustice.org](http://www.restorativejustice.org)

Conclusion

This suggested reading list provides a variety of resources for readers interested in exploring restorative justice and family reunification in greater depth. From foundational texts to advanced readings, practical guides, and specialized topics, these recommendations offer valuable insights and practical knowledge to support the continued growth and development of restorative justice practices. Whether you are a practitioner, scholar, or advocate, these resources will enhance your understanding and effectiveness in promoting healing, accountability, and reconciliation.

www.ingramcontent.com/pod-product-compliance
Ingram Content Group UK Ltd.
Pitfield, Milton Keynes, MK11 3LW, UK
UKHW021708190726
13853UKWH00001B/458

9 798330 323401